THE COMPLETE
WORST-CASE SCENARIO
Survival Handbook:

DATING & SEX

The
COMPLETE
WORST-CASE SCENARIO
Survival Handbook
DATING & SEX

By David Borgenicht, Joshua Piven, & Ben H. Winters

With contributions by Victoria De Silverio, Sarah Jordan,
Turk Regan, Sam Stall, and Jennifer Worick

Illustrations by Brenda Brown

CHRONICLE BOOKS
SAN FRANCISCO

Worst-Case Scenario® and The Worst-Case Scenario Survival Handbook™ are
trademarks of Quirk Productions, Inc.

Library of Congress Cataloging-in-Publication Data

Borgenicht, David.
  The complete worst-case scenario survival handbook : dating & sex / by David
Borgenicht, Joshua Piven & Ben H. Winters ; with contributions by Victoria De
Silverio ... [et al.] ; illustrations by Brenda Brown.
     p. cm.
  Rev. ed. of: The worst-case scenario survival handbook : dating & sex / Joshua
Piven, David Borgenicht and Jennifer Worick. c2001.
  ISBN 978-1-4521-1695-2
  1. Dating (Social customs))—Handbooks, manuals, etc. 2. Dating (Social
customs)—Humor. 3. Sex)—Handbooks, manuals, etc. 4. Sex)—Humor.
5. Man-woman relationships)—Handbooks, manuals, etc. 6. Man-woman
relationships)—Humor. I. Piven, Joshua. II. Winters, Ben H. III. Piven, Joshua.
Worst-case scenario survival handbook. IV. Title. V. Title: Dating & sex.

  HQ801.P597 2013
  306.73--dc23

                                    2012031598

Manufactured in China

Typeset in Adobe Caslon, Bundesbahn Pi, and Zapf Dingbats

Designed by Dennis Gallagher and John Sullivan, www.visdesign.com
Illustrations by Brenda Brown

Visit www.worstcasescenarios.com

10 9 8 7 6 5 4 3 2 1

Chronicle Books LLC
680 Second Street
San Francisco, California 94107
www.chroniclebooks.com

WARNING

When a life is imperiled or a dire situation is at hand, safe alternatives may not exist. To deal with the worst-case scenarios presented in this book, we highly recommend—insist, actually—that the best course of action is to consult a professionally trained expert. But because highly trained professionals may not always be available when the safety or sanity of individuals is at risk, we have asked experts on various subjects to describe the techniques they might employ in these emergency situations. THE AUTHORS, PUBLISHER, AND EXPERTS DISCLAIM ANY LIABILITY from any injury that may result from the use, proper or improper, of the information contained in this book. We do not guarantee that the information contained herein is complete, safe, or accurate for your situation, nor should it be considered a substitute for your good judgment and common sense. And finally, nothing in this book should be construed or interpreted to infringe on the rights of other persons or to violate criminal statutes; we urge you to obey all laws and respect all rights, including property rights, of others.

—The Authors

CONTENTS

7 Wallowing...285

The course of true love never did run smooth.

—William Shakespeare

Love is like racing across the frozen tundra on a
snowmobile which flips over, trapping you underneath.
At night, the ice-weasels come.

—Matt Groening

INTRODUCTION

In nature, the process of finding a mate is a fairly simple one. Animals signal their readiness by fanning their plumage, or changing the color of their buttocks, or growling in a certain way. Potential suitors present themselves, then vie for the right to mate. In nature, there are no singles bars, dating websites, personal ads, safe lunches, or blind dates.

Among humans, however, finding a suitable mate is a lot more complex, and more dangerous. From the first attraction across a crowded room to the perils of meeting, dating, undressing, sleeping with, and loving or leaving that special someone, you are completely at risk: your body, your heart, your mind, and your spirit, not to mention your bank account. Literature and lyrics say it all: Love hurts. Love is blind. Love stinks. Love is a battlefield. Think of this book as your guide to fighting, surviving, and ultimately winning that battle.

We've learned a few things about survival in creating *The Worst-Case Scenario Survival Handbook* series. We've learned how to fend off an alligator, how to survive a jump from a bridge, how to escape from quicksand, and how to survive many other life-threatening situations.

That was the easy part.

It was easy to give readers instructions for surviving the elements or wild animal attacks. It's simple enough to predict what a shark is going to do, or to teach people how to jump from a moving car, or to give readers information about what to do during an earthquake. Sharks are always going to behave like sharks, moving cars are always going to function according to the principles of physics, and earthquakes affect the ground and buildings in a very predictable way. But humans are unpredictable—and you never know how they will react when things take a turn for the worse and especially when love is in the air.

In dating and sex, perhaps more than in any other aspect of life, you've got to be able to cope when things don't work out as planned. If you are careless or you panic, if you say or do the wrong thing or do the right thing at the wrong time, the consequences could be emotionally catastrophic and life-threatening (or life-producing). This book can keep you safe.

There are plenty of books out there that provide guidance on how to find Mr. or Ms. Right. This is the only book that tells you how to escape from Mr. or Ms. Wrong, identify an axe murderer, slip away from a bad date, fake an orgasm, recognize breast implants and toupees, remove difficult articles of clothing, treat a passion injury, apologize when you don't know what you've done wrong, optimize your online dating profile, avoid nightmare hookups, and more. *Much* more. When we published *The Worst-Case Scenario Survival Handbook: Dating & Sex* more than 10 years ago, we set out to give readers answers to more than 40 scenarios. This new complete handbook adds a hundred additional scenarios on love, dating, sex, relationships, and marriage from across the series, including dozens of all new scenarios and expert advice that can save your evening and your love life.

Generally, we've assigned a "he" or "she" to each of the scenarios for the sake of simplicity, but you'll know if the scenario applies to you. And even if it doesn't, you might find out how to help a friend or lover in distress.

And in the handy appendix, you'll find excuses you might need, a guide to pickup lines to avoid, and a body language interpretation chart for encouragement—or for extra protection.

So take heart, love and sex-seekers. This book will provide you with everything you need to navigate the dangerous waters in the sea of love—and avoid what lurks beneath the surface.

—The Authors

CHAPTER 1

DEFENSIVE DATING

HOW TO DETERMINE IF YOUR DATE IS AN AXE MURDERER

1 Watch for the following:
- A Caucasian male in his twenties or thirties
- Obsession with fire or matches
- Cruelty to animals
- History of bed-wetting
- Sexually abused as a child
- Middle-class background combined with loner behavior
- Difficulty maintaining relationships

An individual who exhibits more than three of these traits may be dangerous.

2 Trust your intuition.
Your instinct is a powerful weapon. If something feels wrong, it probably is.

3 Check him out officially.
Obtain his social security number and investigate him. Call the Federal Prison Locator Service (202-307-3126) to determine if he was ever incarcerated. Many online companies can aid in financial reports or tracking down previous addresses. You may also want to enlist the services of a private detective.

Axe murderers are usually Caucasian males in their twenties and thirties. They frequently behave cruelly toward animals and may also be obsessed with fire or matches.

4 If you discover grounds for suspicion, break off the relationship immediately.

Be clear and definite about your decision. Return all of his belongings and gifts. Do not make promises to keep in touch. Be straightforward and kind, and talk only about yourself and why the relationship no longer works for you. Do not blame him. Try not to make him angry.

5 Take steps to maintain your safety.
- Carry a cell phone.
- Install a home security system.
- Change your phone numbers.
- Stay near populated, well-lit areas.
- Apprise a friend or relative of your concerns.
- Document any strange or unusual happenings.
- Take a personal safety/self-defense class.

HOW TO
DETERMINE IF YOUR
DATE IS MARRIED

1 Examine the left ring finger.
After a period of about one year, a wedding band leaves a circle of lighter skin around the base of the ring finger. Your date may also touch the base of that finger inadvertently, as if something is missing.

2 Ask for a home phone number.
Most people in committed relationships spend at least one or two hours a week on the phone; if your date will not give you his home phone number, then he is worried someone else will answer when you call.

3 Insist on holding hands when walking in public.
If your date is interested and attracted to you, then he will not object to such a small and commonplace display of affection—unless he fears that someone will spot you together.

4 Search your date's car.
The automobile registration may be in the spouse's name, or in both names. It is usually kept in the glove compartment, behind the sun visor or, for non-smokers, in the ashtray. Look for signs of a spouse (clothing, makeup) or other indicators (pacifiers, pieces of crackers, toys) of a family your date has not mentioned.

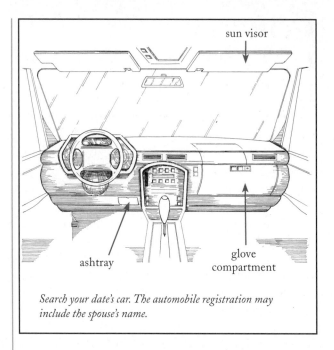

Search your date's car. The automobile registration may include the spouse's name.

5 Ask to meet some of his friends.

After two or three dates, this is not an unusual request. If your date claims that his friends remain close to his ex-wife, or that it's too soon to bring you into their social circle, you have good reason to believe that you are not the only woman in his life.

6 Invite him to spend the night.

If you have engaged in sexual activity on several occasions but he always refuses to stay the night, then he very likely has someone waiting for him.

7 | Make plans to spend a weekend together.
If you never see him on Saturdays and Sundays, be suspicious. Your date may say that he spends weekends with his parents and/or with his children. But if he cares so much for you, and if his family is as great as he says they are, they will understand if you come along or if he shares time on the weekends with you.

8 | Ask to meet his children.
He might have legitimate reasons for not introducing you to his children early in the relationship—for example, he may not want to present you as a possible mommy replacement until the relationship becomes more serious. However, it may also mean he is still married to their mommy.

Be Aware

- Be suspicious of a lover who never writes you letters or sends e-mails, and signs greeting cards with only a nickname, an initial, or a term of endearment. This person may be making a conscious effort to avoid any paper trails to the relationship. For this same reason, also be wary of a date who always pays cash (see "How to Have an Affair and Not Get Caught," page page 245).

HOW TO DETERMINE THE GENDER OF YOUR DATE

1 Look at her (or his) hand.
Compare the length of your date's fourth and second fingers. Most men have ring fingers that are conspicuously longer than their index fingers, whereas most women have ring fingers that are close to the same length. Testosterone levels likely account for the greater length.

Also take notice of the amount of hair on your date's knuckles, hands, and forearms. Most men will have visible, dark hair (or signs of recently removed hair) on their hands and wrists, and sometimes knuckles.

2 Be suspicious of baggy clothing.
Your date may be trying to conceal a telltale bulge.

3 Look for an Adam's apple.
Most men have a bump in the middle of their throat. Most women do not.

4 Observe shoulders and hips.
Men's shoulders tend to be broader than their hips, while women's hips and shoulders tend to be closer to the same width. Do not be fooled by shoulder pads.

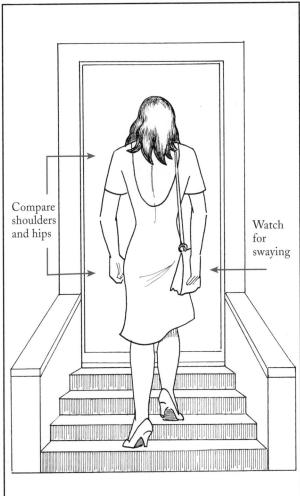

Compare shoulders and hips

Watch for swaying

Men's shoulders tend to be broader than their hips, while women's hips and shoulders tend to be closer to the same width. When ascending stairs, women tend to sway more than men.

5 Follow your date up a flight of stairs.
Take note of how she (or he) moves while ascending. Men tend to walk in a more "straight ahead" motion with minimal "wobbling" back and forth. Women tend to sway a bit from side to side, due to the position of their pelvises. Women also tend to lean forward slightly.

Be Aware

- Look for at least three of these characteristics before you draw conclusions about your date's gender, then make your plans accordingly.
- Voice is not always a good indicator of gender—a low voice may simply be the result of hard living.

HOW TO DETERMINE IF YOUR DATE IS A CON ARTIST

1 Watch for the following:
- Has your date missed a string of dates with you?
- Does she change dates at the last minute?
- Does she frequently receive unexplained phone calls?
- Does she refuse to give out information about her past?
- Is she known only by a first or last name?
- Is she loath to contact family members?
- Does she lack connections to the community, friends, or co-workers?
- Does she frequently express concerns about her finances?
- Has she ever asked you for a short-term loan or investment?
- Does she often change her stories and claims?

If the answer to three or more of these questions is yes, you may be dating a con artist (or a pathological liar).

2 Watch your date's eyes during conversation.
Most people look to their right when recalling the truth, the past, and events that actually happened.

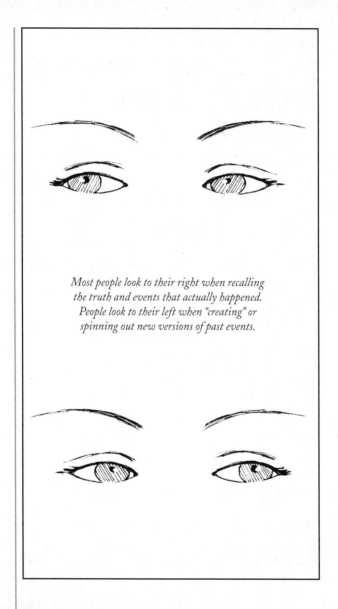

Most people look to their right when recalling
the truth and events that actually happened.
People look to their left when "creating" or
spinning out new versions of past events.

People look to the left when "creating" or spinning out new versions of past events. Ask her a question about her past and see where her eyes move.

3 Obtain her social security number and investigate her records.

With a social security number or driver's license number and birthdate, you can check out a person's records—criminal, financial, voting, and more. A good place to start is a "people finder" website on the Internet. Or you can hire a private detective.

4 Trust your intuition.

If you have doubts, there is probably a reason.

5 Protect yourself.

Take an inventory of your credit cards, bank accounts, and other financial assets. If you have broken off the relationship and she is desperate, she may try to dupe or rob you. Request new credit cards; change your e-mail, voicemail, burglar alarm, and banking passwords; select a new PIN for each of your accounts. Change your locks, if necessary.

HOW TO FEND OFF AN OBSESSIVE EX

1 Make your rejection final and firm.

Do not give your ex a chance to manipulate or negotiate. Refuse all offers for dates, favors, and "friendly meetings." Express your wish to be left alone. Make sure your body language sends the same message. Do not touch during the rejection, but look your ex firmly in the eyes.

2 Do not discuss the past.

Never mention the good times you had together. Instead, speak enthusiastically about how happy you are now, and make it clear that you have moved on with your life.

3 Immediately sever all ties.

Return all of your ex's belongings (including any gifts to you) in one shipment. Do not prolong the process. If your ex continues to call, get a new, unlisted phone number. Do not call or send cards, letters, or e-mails; these will result in a mixed message and may give your ex hope of reconciliation.

4 If your ex will not leave you alone, sound a warning.

At the first sign that your ex is not listening to you, announce that if the unwanted behavior persists, you will take action. Threaten to contact the authorities, and be prepared to do so. Do not give in to any threats that may come your way. Be ready to secure a restraining order or civil protection order if it becomes necessary for your peace of mind.

5 Inform your family, friends, and co-workers about the situation.
Having larger, stronger friends around may serve as a deterrent.

6 Keep a paper trail.
You may need evidence later. Save any relevant letters, notes, e-mails, and voicemails—anything that can prove unwanted attention. Maintain a log or diary of your ex's actions and report any unlawful behavior to the police immediately. Report phone calls from your ex to both the phone company and the police. Write down your caller ID log, if you have one.

7 Inform the authorities.
Do not let fear of retribution stop you from taking action. If your ex persists in contacting you, becomes easily enraged by your rejections, is overly interested in your private life, or shows up in unexpected locations, he or she has become a stalker. Take legal action immediately and obtain a restraining order.

8 Move.
Make sure that your new address is unlisted. Contact the department of motor vehicles and the voter registration bureau to have them block your address. Forward your mail to a P.O. box, and do not accept any packages unless you are certain who sent them.

9 Take steps to preserve your safety.

Get a cell phone and carry it with you at all times. Consider getting a guard dog and taking self-defense classes.

Be Aware

- If your ex shows up where you work, notify co-workers of the situation and vary the times you come and go from work. If possible, have someone accompany you as you approach the building.

HOW TO FEND OFF A PICKUP ARTIST

1   Recognize the traits of a pickup artist.
Is your suitor overly charming and quick with cash? Does he appear to have an immediate connection with you? Is he scanning the room while talking to you? Is he calling you familiar or condescending names such as "honey," "sweetie," or "babe"?

2   Do not accept drinks.
Letting a pickup artist buy you drinks will encourage him and make him feel he is entitled to your attentions.

3   Keep personal information to yourself.
Do not give him your name, and do not tell him where you live, who you are waiting for, or any other detail or insight into your personal life or plans.

4   Make it clear that you are not interested.
Be direct and forceful. If he persists, you may have to become rude or leave. If you make it obvious that nothing is going to happen that evening, he'll move on to other prospects.

5   Turn away and ignore him.
Talk to a friend or the person sitting on the other side of you. The pickup artist likes the chase most of all— put a stop to the chase and he will look elsewhere.

The Elbow Knock: Turn back to glance at the pickup artist and sweep your elbow toward the glass.

The Time Check: Turn your wrist to look at your watch, and spill your drink on the pickup artist.

6 Cause an "accident."

- The Elbow Knock: Use this technique if you are seated at a bar or table. Notice where glasses and plates are located on your table. Turn around to talk to a friend, or simply look away, and position your elbow. As you turn back, sweep your elbow into any glasses or plates on the table, knocking them into his lap or onto his shirt.

- The Hair Flip: While standing facing your suitor, bring your hand up to adjust your hair. Do this quickly so that he tips his glass toward his body and his drink spills all over him.

- The Time Check: While standing next to your would-be suitor, hold your drink in the hand of your watch arm. Say, "Is it [*time*] yet?" Then turn your wrist to look at your watch, thereby spilling the drink on the pickup artist.

7 Apologize insincerely.

HOW TO DEAL WITH A DATE WHO MOVES TOO FAST

1 Watch for the signs of "relationship acceleration."
If your date starts talking about moving in or having kids or marrying, and you are not yet ready to proceed that quickly, you may have a problem.

2 Tell your date to slow down.
Send a clear, unambiguous message. Sometimes joking about it will convey your feelings, but if a light touch does not work, express it more directly: tell him that you think he is getting too serious too soon, and that you think you both should spend time with other friends.

3 Do not agree to more than one date a week.
By no means should you plan a weekend vacation together.

4 Talk about past relationships.
Find out what goals he had in recent relationships. Someone who moves at a lightning pace may be on the rebound, wanting only to replace a past relationship. Be sure you are not being used merely as a vehicle for accomplishing a goal that you were not involved in setting, like having kids or buying a house.

5 Postpone any conversation about the future of your relationship.

If you want to continue dating this person but do not want to get serious yet, suggest discussing the situation at a specific date in the future, after you have spent some more time together.

6 Beware of flattery.

When someone wants to move too fast, he may just be lonely or incapable of being single. You may feel flattered by his seriousness, but often his intensity does not have much to do with you. He may only want to be with someone, anyone.

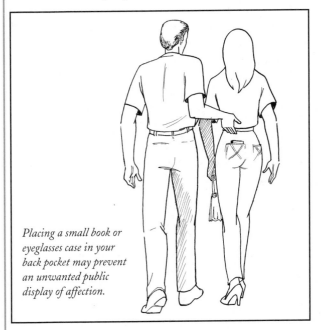

Placing a small book or eyeglasses case in your back pocket may prevent an unwanted public display of affection.

How to Stop Unwanted PDA

Overeager dates may use a Public Display of Affection (PDA) to accelerate a relationship, unaware that these PDAs may make you, your friends, or even casual bystanders feel uncomfortable. The best solution is to voice discomfort—but because that can be awkward, use the following techniques to block an unwanted PDA:

- Handholding: If your date tries to hold your hand, allow him to do so for a few minutes, release the hand to adjust your hair, and then lower the hand to your side. Alternative: You could fake a sneeze, then lower both hands to your sides.

- Kissing: As your date advances, step back and explain you're catching a cold. Sound concerned for your date's health and well-being. Alternative: Sneeze or cough in his face.

- Walking with One Hand Slipped in the Rear Pocket of Your Pants: Pull your date's hand out of your pocket, perhaps with a coy line like, "Wait until we get home." Alternative: Place an object—a checkbook, a wallet, a folded scarf, a glasses case, or a rolled newspaper—in the pocket.

HOW TO ESCAPE FROM A BAD DATE

Fake an Emergency

1 Excuse yourself from the table.
Tell your date that you are going to the restroom to "wash up." Take your cell phone with you. If you do not have one, locate a restaurant phone that's out of your date's line of vision. Bring a restaurant matchbook or a business card that includes the restaurant's phone number.

2 Call a friend or relative for help.
Tell them to call you (either on your cell phone or on the restaurant's phone) and pretend there has been an emergency. Believable emergencies are:
- Personal Crisis: "My friend just broke up with her husband—she's having a breakdown. I have to go."
- Business Crisis: "My boss just called—she's in Seattle for a major presentation, and has lost all her files. I have to e-mail them to her immediately."
- Health Crisis: "My sister just called—our grandmother is alone and ill."

3 Leave quickly before your date can protest.
Apologize, but refuse any attempt your date makes to accompany you. If you leave swiftly and without hesitation, your date won't have time to understand what's happening or to object.

SLIP AWAY UNNOTICED

1 Identify your escape route.
Observe your surroundings. Take note of the exits, especially the back doors. Look for the best way out and an alternative.

2 Plan to alter your appearance.
Think about your most distinctive features and figure out how to hide or disguise them. The person you are trying to leave is going to see a figure moving past and away at a distance and will be focusing on the first impression. If you are not familiar to him and are uninteresting, you will not get a second look.

3 Excuse yourself from the table.
Move to the restroom or any private area with a mirror to begin your transformation. Your date will probably wait only two or three minutes before expecting you to return, so act quickly, before he begins looking for you.

4 Add or remove clothing.
Layering garments will change your body shape and even suggest a different gender. A long coat will obscure your body type. Hats are especially useful because they conceal your hair and facial features. Eyeglasses, whether added or removed, work wonders. A shopping bag is a handy prop and can be used to hold your belongings.

Add—or remove—eyeglasses. Roll or unroll your sleeves; tuck in or untuck your blouse. Modify your hairstyle.

5 Change your walk and posture.
If you usually walk quickly, move slowly. If you stand up straight, hunch over. To alter your gait, slip a pebble in one shoe or bind one of your knees with a piece of string or cloth.

6 Use or remove cosmetics.
Lipstick can change the shape of your mouth, heighten the color in your cheeks and nose, and even give you tired eyes if dabbed and blended on your eyelids. An eyebrow pencil can be used to add age lines, change the shape of your eyes and brows, or create facial hair.

7 Change your hairstyle or color.
A rubber band, hairspray, water, or any gooey substance can be useful for changing a hairstyle, darkening your hair, or altering a hairline. Borrow flour from the kitchen to lighten or gray your hair color.

8 Adopt a cover role.
A waiter in the restaurant may have an apron and be carrying a tray. If you can manage to procure these items, add or subtract a pair of eyeglasses and alter your hairline or hairstyle, you can become invisible as you are moving out of the restaurant, into the kitchen, and out the rear door. Or you can take on the role of a maintenance worker; carry a convenient potted plant out the front door and no one will think twice.

9 Make your move.
Do not look at your date.

If you do not think you will be able to change your appearance enough to slip past your date, you may have to find another way to depart. Back doors are the simplest; they are often located near the rest-rooms or are marked as fire exits. Do not open an emergency exit door if it is alarmed unless absolutely necessary; an alarm will only draw attention. If there are no accessible alternate doors, you will need to find a window.

1 Locate a usable window.
Avoid windows with chicken wire or large plate glass. Bathroom windows often work best. If you are not on the ground floor, be sure there is a fire escape.

2 Attempt to open the window.
Do not immediately break the window, no matter how dire your need to get out.

3 Prepare to break the window if you cannot open it.
Make sure no one is around. If you can, lock the bathroom door.

4 Find an implement to break the window.
Try to avoid using your elbow, fist, or foot. Suitable implements are:
- Wastebasket
- Toilet plunger
- Handbag or briefcase
- Paper towel dispenser

Strike the center of the glass with the implement.

5 Strike the center of the glass with the implement.
If the hand holding the implement will come within
a foot of the window as you break it, wrap it with a
jacket or sweater before attempting to break the glass.
If no implement is available, use your heavily wrapped
hand; be sure you wrap your arm as well, beyond the
elbow.

6 | Punch out any remaining shards of glass.
Cover your fist with a jacket or sweater before removing the glass.

7 | Make your escape.
Do not worry about any minor nicks and cuts. Run.

Get Your Date to Leave

1 | Say something offensive.
If you know your date is of a particular religion or ethnicity, make inappropriate comments.

2 | Behave inappropriately.
Do things that you think he will find unattractive or distasteful: chew with your mouth open, eat with your fingers, argue with the waiter, close your eyes and pretend to sleep, light matches and drop them on your plate, ignore everything he says, and/or call someone else on your cell phone.

3 | Send your date on a "fool's errand."
- Tell him you want to go to a specific nightclub, but explain that it gets very crowded and that if you are not in line by a certain time (say, fifteen minutes from then), you won't get in. Tell your date that you have arranged to have your friend stop by the restaurant with guest passes, but that if your date does not go ahead to the nightclub to get in line, you'll never make it inside. If your date wants your cell phone number, give the number willingly but make

sure you change one digit. Promise you will see your date within half an hour. Never show.

- Fake an allergy attack, and insist that he leave in search of the appropriate over-the-counter allergy medicine. Explain that you must have been allergic to something in the drink/appetizer/food/taxicab, and that if you do not obtain your medicine you will break out in hives. When your date dutifully leaves, slip away.

Be Aware

- Blind dates are the riskiest form of dating—it is best to check out a potential suitor extensively before the date.
- Have a friend agree to check out your potential suitor and call you before you enter the bar/restaurant. Send your friend in with a cell phone. Situate yourself at a bar nearby, and await her call. Have her contact you when she has identified the mark.
- If you discover unsavory facts about someone you're supposed to meet, call immediately to cancel the date. Blame work and say that you have to stay late at the office, or say that you're experiencing car trouble. A more permanent solution is to say that an old flame has reentered your life; this will prevent your blind date from calling you again and asking for a rain check.

HOW TO SURVIVE IF YOU HAVE NO ONE TO KISS ON NEW YEAR'S EVE

IF YOU ARE WITH OTHERS

1 Keep a glass in your hand.
If others think you are being festive and uninhibited, you are much more likely to receive a kiss. Even if you are not drinking, always hold a partly full glass of champagne.

2 Hug people.
As the clock strikes midnight, begin hugging everyone around you.

3 Select a desirable person.
As you are hugging, look for an attractive person who you would enjoy kissing and who might kiss you. If a person is not randomly kissing others, he or she may be less likely to kiss you.

4 Begin your approach.
Act casual, but keep your destination in view. Slowly move toward your chosen one, hugging everyone on the way.

5 | Time your arrival.
Do not appear to be "lining up" to kiss this person. Time your arrival precisely as the person releases the previous reveler.

6 | Yell first, then hug.
Yell "Happy New Year!" as you move in. Hug, embrace, then pull away slightly.

7 | Kiss.
Keep your mouth closed, pucker slightly, and plant the kiss.

IF YOU ARE ALONE

1 | Kiss a pet.
Dogs are generally agreeable and have relatively clean mouths. Cats are usually well groomed but are more passive and tend to get rather than give. Keep your mouth closed.

2 | Kiss yourself.
Find a mirror, pucker up, lean close, and kiss. Keep the lips slightly parted. Do not attempt to use your tongue. Wipe the mirror clean after you have completed your kiss. You may also try kissing the back of your hand.

3 | Kiss a celebrity.
Watch a favorite movie or show on television and kiss the screen when an appealing star has a close-up. Wipe

If no humans are available to kiss at midnight, try kissing a pet. Keep your mouth closed.

the screen first to remove dust and static electricity, and wipe the screen after to remove any evidence.

4 Hug a pillow.
Full-body pillows are more satisfying.

5 Call a friend on the phone.
After you wish your friend a happy New Year, give the telephone mouthpiece loud, smacking kisses. (This works less well with cellular phones.)

HOW TO FEND OFF AN UNWANTED HOLIDAY KISS

On Arrival

1 Carry a present, coat, hat, or child in front of you as you enter.

2 Extend your free arm in a wide arc and move into a hug position.

3 If the greeter leans in to plant a kiss, use the head-and-shoulders maneuver.
Move your head toward the kisser, then at the last moment, rotate your shoulders, throw your arm around, and bury your head in the kisser's neck.

Under the Mistletoe

1 Find the mistletoe.
As soon as you arrive, determine the location of the mistletoe. Check the lintel over doorways and hanging lights, which often obscure the mistletoe.

2 Establish alternate routes.
Avoiding the mistletoe is the best defense. Plan your comings and goings so that you do not pass under the mistletoe.

Carry a large present in your arms as you enter in order to block an unwanted kiss.

3 Employ evasive maneuvers.

If the mistletoe is hung in an inescapable location and someone is approaching, be prepared to use counter-measures:

- Keep walking, as if you didn't realize you were under the mistletoe.
- Carry a drink or plate of food at all times, and quickly take a sip or bite as the person approaches.

- Sneeze, cough, or scratch your nose just as the person moves in. When they hesitate, turn the attempted kiss into a friendly hug.
- Move rapidly and place a preemptive, glancing kiss on the person's forehead or cheek, thereby avoiding a more serious kiss.

4 Make up a mistletoe-related fib.

When fleeing from the would-be kisser seems too rude and other defensive tactics won't work, create a new mistletoe custom that would preclude the kiss:

- "This mistletoe has no berries! That's bad luck!"
- "That's not real mistletoe, it's plastic! How tacky—we can't kiss under that!"
- "Can you believe they put up mistletoe? Who believes in that anymore?"

Be Aware

- Portable mistletoe—a sprig attached to the end of a curved stick—is not valid mistletoe and does not invoke the kiss tradition. (You might also question why you are attending a party with someone who would attempt the "mistletoe-on-a-stick" trick.)
- Do not attempt to avoid a mistletoe kiss by claiming that you are not Christian. The custom of kissing under mistletoe is not specific to Christianity and is observed in many religions and countries.

HOW TO SURVIVE A WORKPLACE ROMANCE

★ **Do not tell colleagues.**
Do not discuss any aspect of your relationship with anyone at work, even close friends. Avoid telltale references, such as, "When we were at the movies last night . . ." Do not play guessing games with co-workers, such as, "I'm going out with someone from the office but you'll never guess who."

★ **Resist physical contact at the office.**
Avoid all physical contact, including kissing, hand-holding, hugging, casual touching, and back rubs, even if you think you are alone. Maintain at least a foot of personal space between you and the person you are dating.

★ **Send gifts to the home.**
Do not have flowers, candy, clothing, or other personal items sent to the office, even with an unsigned card: People will begin asking questions.

★ **Do not use company e-mail to send personal notes.**
Many employers monitor e-mail messages, and even deleted messages are stored. It is also too easy to send an e-mail to the wrong person or to "everyone."

Avoid physical contact in the office, even when you think no one else is looking.

✪ Avoid long or excessive lunch dates.
While it is acceptable for colleagues to eat togeth-er, extended or repeated outings may attract notice. Maintain the lunch routine you practiced before you started dating your co-worker.

✪ Avoid arriving and departing together.
Unless you are in a car pool with others, stagger your arrival and departure times.

✪ Use discretion.
At company picnics or parties, or at off-site meetings, do not drink excessively, dance intimately, or openly display affection with your office significant other.

Be Aware

- Most office romances begin in the spring.
- Dating more than one person from the same company at the same time is not a good idea.

THE BREAK-UP

✪ **Do not break up at work.**
Emotions can be difficult to hide, and people can act irrationally when they are upset. The workplace, especially in a cubicle but even in a private office, is a poor choice of location for a confrontation. Avoid breaking up over lunch hour, as well.

✪ **Break up over a long weekend.**
Choose a time when your partner will have several days to heal before having to see you at the office. Try to be sensitive to his or her feelings, however: Do not break up just before the other person leaves on an extended vacation.

✪ **Be prepared for the worst.**
A bad break-up may require you to transfer or even resign, particularly if you are dating someone above you in the office hierarchy. Ending a relationship with someone who reports to you could lead to a charge of sexual discrimination.

✪ Do not immediately begin dating someone else at work.
Your new relationship may be hurtful to your ex, if you are spotted. You may also gain a reputation for being opportunistic or desperate.

✪ Do not discuss personal feelings or emotions with your ex while at work.
If you want to check on how your former lover is doing, call the person at home.

Be Aware
* No matter what you call it—fishing off the company pier, mentoring the intern, kissing company cousins, refilling the toner, mergers and acquisitions—office romances are dangerous.

HOW TO DATE A VAMPIRE IF YOU ARE A "MORNING PERSON"

✪ Let him sleep.
Depending on what strain of vampirism your partner is cursed with, sunlight may be unpleasant, harmful, or outright fatal to him, and thus his life is likely oriented around the nighttime hours. When you are ready to wake up and start the day, your vampire will still be sleeping off a long night of bloodfeast. Go for a solitary jog or curl up with the paper until he's ready to arise.

✪ Be respectful.
Don't perform loud activities, such as vacuuming (which can wake a vampire) or ringing church bells (which can destroy one).

✪ Demand respect in return.
If his entry and exit from his coffin are loud and disrupt your sleep, ask for consideration as he moves about in the dead of night.

✪ Sleep separately.
Intimate relationships do not necessarily require sleeping in the same bed. You take the cozy bedroom; he has his coffin filled with cemetery dirt in the basement.

✪ Experiment.
Explore your mutual interest in vampires through daylight-safe indoor activities such as hosting your own vampire film festival, comparing and discussing the creatures' depiction in various movies and TV shows. What did they get right? What did they get wrong?

✪ Find mutually agreeable times for togetherness.
Go for walks together in the last purple hour of daylight, when the sun is slowly sinking, before you get too tired and he is compelled to feed.

✪ Communicate with notes.
Slip an affectionate message, such as "I love you—happy hunting!" into the fold of his cape to remind him even when he's at work that you're thinking of him.

✪ Reorient your sleep schedule.
The human circadian rhythm can be retrained to sleep during the day and wake at night; consider changing your habits to match those of your vampire partner. The key is regularity: Stay up all night the first time, go to sleep at dawn in a dark room, and make yourself stick to that pattern, resisting the impulse to get out of bed during midday, until it feels natural to wake fresh in the early evening every day.

✪ Use his powers.
Many vampires have the ability to appear in dreams. Ask your vampire to visit you in your dreams.

Be aware of loud activities that could disrupt a vampire's sleep.

how to date a vampire if you are a "morning person"

HOW TO SURVIVE A LOVE TRIANGLE WITH A WEREWOLF AND A VAMPIRE

1 Juggle.

Use a calendar to block off the best times to be with each creature according to its own infernal cycles. Plan dates with the werewolf for nights with a waning moon so that he's not preoccupied with the physical challenges of transformation; with the vampire, schedule together time on nights with a fuller moon and for just after he has recently feasted, when he will be sated and more ready to engage in other activities.

2 Take your time.

Both partners enjoy eternal life, so don't feel rushed to make up your mind for their sakes.

3 Be honest.

When either relationship becomes serious, inform each creature that you are involved with the other and make clear the priority in which you hold the relationship.

4 Avoid scenes.

Both werewolves and vampires possess ferocious animal instincts and are quick to anger. Try not to let them encounter the other, especially in your presence.

Plan your calendar to avoid crossing the nocturnal schedules of your vampire and werewolf companions.

5 Find a nice human boy.
Break up with both monsters. Move to a new town and pray for your own safety and that of your new beau.

HOW TO BREAK UP WITH A VAMPIRE

1 Brood dramatically.
Pace the floors of the castle. Stare up at the cold light of the moon. Sigh, moan, and curse the day you ever met him.

2 Weigh the pros and cons.
Confirm that you have made the right decision by making a list of plusses and minuses to continuing the relationship. List as many cons (e.g., committed to evil) as possible. For any pros (e.g., promise of eternal life), are there downsides (e.g., eternal boredom)?

3 Pick a good time.
Don't break up with the vampire on Valentine's Day, his birthday or rebirth day, or when he hasn't feasted for several days.

4 Look away.
It can be hard to maintain your nerve while staring into the literally mesmerizing eyes of a vampire. Close your eyes, or look out the window, while telling him how you feel.

5 Be brief and direct.
As with any breakup, your goal is to tell the truth without being overly informative. Say your piece and then stop speaking.

6 | Don't make it about the vampirism.
Find other reasons to explain the breakup, such as his personal habits or friends, rather than the fact that he is a heartless, shape-shifting destroyer of men.

7 | Be firm.
The vampire may protest, saying that he can change. Remind yourself that he's been alive for many centuries and genuine change is unlikely.

8 | Keep it about the two of you.
If you have fallen for someone else, do not mention it; vampires are notorious seekers of vengeance.

9 | Skip the goodbye kiss.

How to Get Over a Vampire

1 | Give yourself time.
A good rule of thumb is that getting over someone takes half the length of time as the relationship itself. If you've been dating the vampire for countless millennia, count on a similarly epic grieving period.

2 | Remove evidence of the vampire from your life.
Don't listen to his favorite songs; throw away his old capes; scrub the bloodstains from around the house.

3 | Focus on the bad times.
When you think of the vampire, remember the tedious nights spent traipsing through graveyards, and how cold and distant he could be.

Chapter 2

FIRST IMPRESSIONS

HOW TO SPOT A FAKE

Breast Implants

1 Remember: if they look too good to be true, they probably are.

If a woman is over thirty and her breasts defy gravity without a bra or she has a strikingly full and firm upper cleavage and bosom, chances are her breasts are not fully natural. You should also be suspicious of breasts that sit very high on a woman's chest; this is another good sign of implants.

2 Assess breast size as compared to frame size.

Most, though not all, petite women have naturally small breasts.

3 Be suspicious of baseball-shaped breasts or strangely arranged breasts.

In cases of a poor augmentation, the outline of the implant may be noticeable, or the breast may have a very firm, round, baseball-like appearance. Poorly placed implants can often be seen through tight tops. While a good augmentation procedure can be difficult to detect by visual inspection alone, a bad one is quite noticeable.

4 Check cleavage for rippling of the skin.

Implants may ripple in the cleavage or on top of the breasts; look for a wave pattern across the surface.

If a woman is over thirty and has strikingly full breasts that sit very high on her chest, you have reason to be suspicious.

Natural breasts, even very large breasts, although soft, will never have a rippled appearance.

5 If appropriate, brush up against or hug someone with suspected breast implants.
If her breasts feel firmer than normal, implants may be in use.

6 Check under and around the breast for scarring.
In an intimate situation, the opportunity may arise for a closer visual and tactile inspection. Look for scarring under the breasts, around the nipple, and in the armpit area.

TOUPEES

1 Look for uneven hair texture.
Since toupees do not cover the entire scalp like a wig does, there will always be a place where the real hair meets the purchased hairpiece. Generally, men who wear toupees have thinning hair, so look for a patch of thick hair surrounded by areas with thinner coverage.

2 Beware of an abnormally thick patch of hair on the top of the scalp.
Toupees are very thick in order to effectively cover the nylon or fabric cap that is attached to the scalp.

3 Watch for inconsistent coloring.
Toupees generally do not perfectly match the color of the hair surrounding them. A very dark area of hair surrounded by thinner, lighter hair may indicate a toupee.

4 Note any shifting of hair on the scalp.
Toupees are usually attached to the scalp with wig tape or special adhesive, which can come loose, especially during high winds or excessive perspiration. A patch of hair that has moved or is out of place is a sure sign of a toupee.

5 Test your theory.
Reach for your date's head, saying, "You've got something in your hair." If he reacts quickly to stop you from touching his hair, you may have found a toupee.

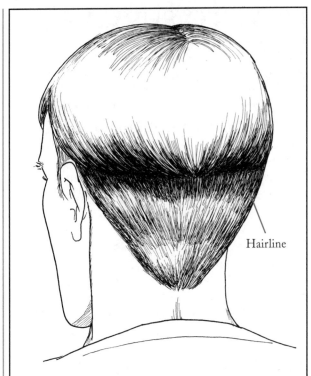

Hairline

Because toupees do not cover the entire scalp, there will always be a place where the real hair meets the purchased hairpiece.

Be Aware

- Many men with thinning hair choose hair plugs, which are hair follicles that have been surgically implanted in the scalp. Lots of small bumps that resemble knots at the base of the hair shafts are a good indicator of hair plugs.

HOW TO SURVIVE A FASHION EMERGENCY

SHIRT CAUGHT IN ZIPPER

1 Grasp the shirttail.
For internal snags, slide your hand inside the front of the pants above the zipper area. Otherwise, hold the material that is sticking out.

2 Pull the stuck fabric taut and upward.

3 Guide the zipper down with your free hand.
Apply steady force to the zipper: pull but don't yank too hard. Be careful not to pinch your fingers. Also, be sure to keep the garment away from the body, so the teeth of the zipper don't bite your skin. This is especially important if you're not wearing underwear.

SPLASHED BY A TAXI

✪ If you are splashed with water, head for the nearest restroom and use the hot-air hand dryer. Stand very close to the dryer and rock from side to side, using your hands to billow and fluff whichever garment is wet.

✪ If you are splattered with mud, add a dash of salt to a glass of club soda from the closest bar and dab it onto

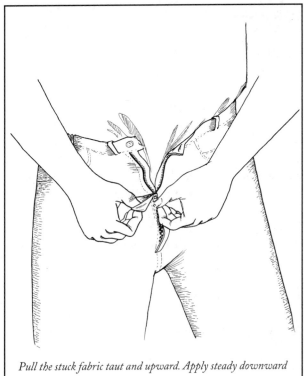

Pull the stuck fabric taut and upward. Apply steady downward force to the zipper.

the dirty spots. The soda will work on the mud; the salt will lift out any oil from the street that was mixed in with the mud.

⭐ If you are wearing a skirt, turn it around so that the splash is less visible. Untuck a shirt or blouse to cover a splashed skirt or pants.

Wine Stain

⭐ For white wine, wet a cloth napkin with cold water and dab the stain. Avoid hot water, which will set the stain.

⭐ For red wine, soak a cloth napkin with white wine and apply to the stain area. Then dab the stain with cool water.

⭐ Rub toothpaste—the white, pasty kind only—onto the stain to make it easier to clean later.

⭐ If you spilled the wine on your date, apologize, offer to pay the dry cleaning bill, and immediately pour or order another glass of wine.

Lipstick Stain

⭐ Apply a generous amount of petroleum jelly to the spot. Baby wipes or wet towelettes will also remove most of the stain. Dry clean as soon as possible.

⭐ Use a scarf to camouflage the area, unless it is on your date's pants.

Ripped Stocking

★ Use clear nail polish or a spritz of hairspray to keep the run from spreading.

★ If the rip is at the toe, stretch the toe out further and tuck the excess fabric under your foot so that the rip cannot be seen.

★ If the rip is down the front, twist your pantyhose to your inner thigh so that the tear is less visible. Be careful as you twist to avoid ripping it further. Or put the hose on backwards, as long as they are not seamed or embellished.

★ As a last resort, remove the stockings and go bare-legged.

HOW TO TREAT
A PIMPLE

1 | Apply a warm compress.
Soak a hand towel in hot water, then hold it against the pimple for a minute or more.

2 | Apply a topical medication.
Use any over-the-counter benzoyl peroxide product.

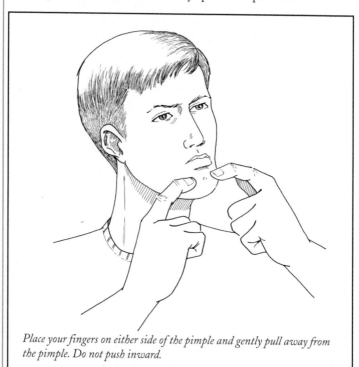

Place your fingers on either side of the pimple and gently pull away from the pimple. Do not push inward.

3 | Do not touch.
Leave the pimple alone for as long as possible.

4 | Reassess the situation.
Immediately before your date, determine if the pimple has come to a head. If so, proceed to step 5.

5 | Pop the pimple.
Place your fingers on either side of the pimple and gently pull away from the pimple. Do not push inward. The pimple will expel its contents if it is ready to, but no harm will be done if it is not.

6 | Apply a cover-up.
Dab the now-empty pimple gently with a tissue to remove any remaining liquid. Apply any cosmetic with a green tint, which will conceal a pimple or the red mark left from a popped pimple (red and green are complementary colors and will negate each other).

HOW TO TREAT A SHAVING WOUND

Minor Cut

1 Rinse the cut with clean, cold water.

2 Apply alum salts or talcum powder.
Alum, a mineral sometimes sold as styptic powder or a styptic pencil, stops blood flow. Hold the alum in place for 10 to 20 seconds, depending on the severity of the wound. While effective, this technique can be painful, since it is literally applying "salt to the wound." The quickly dried cut may also form a noticeable scab. Alternatively, apply a liberal coating of talcum powder to the cut. Although slightly messier than alum, talcum is considerably less painful and will conceal the nicks and cuts. If alum or talcum powder are not available, proceed to step 3.

3 Apply toilet paper.
Tear off a tiny piece of toilet paper or tissue and press it onto the cut for at least 15 seconds, until it adheres by itself.

4 Wait a few minutes.

5 Remove the toilet paper.
Moisten the paper before carefully pulling it from the cut. If it is not moistened, the paper may reopen the cut when you peel it off.

Major Laceration

Most serious shaving wounds occur to the neck, underneath the nose, or underneath an earlobe. The steps below focus on a neck laceration, but can apply to a major wound anywhere.

1 Apply firm pressure directly over the wound.
Place your fingertips at the point where the bleeding seems to be most severe.

2 If the bleeding stops, continue the pressure for an additional 10 minutes.
Remain still until the bleeding subsides. Then go to an emergency room.

3 If the bleeding does not stop, do not panic.
You probably have slowed the flow enough to have time for the next steps.

4 Pinch and hold the bleeding area.
Use your dominant thumb and index finger to pinch the skin where the blood flow is coming from. This will most likely close the vessel even if you cannot see it and will stop the serious bleeding.

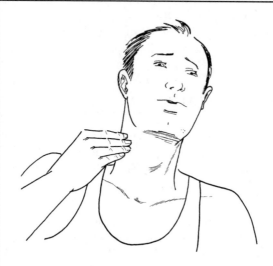

Apply firm pressure directly over the wound. Place your finger-tips at the point where the bleeding seems to be most severe.

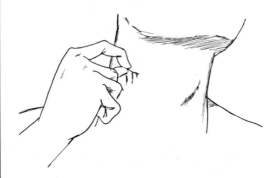

Pushing above or below the site will help seal the area where blood vessels enter the wound.

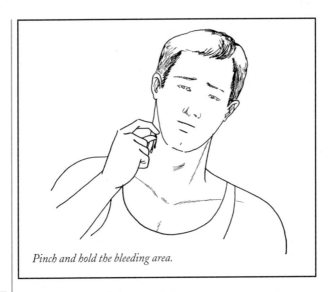

Pinch and hold the bleeding area.

5 Locate the bleeding vessel.

If the bleeding continues despite the steps above, use a piece of cloth or tissue to help you find the exact location of the cut vessel. Carefully ease off the finger pressure while wiping blood away from the wound with the cloth. This should make it easier to see the end of the cut vessel, or to pinpoint its location even if it is deep under the skin. When you see it, try pinching it again.

6 Apply pressure directly above and below the bleeding site.

If bleeding is still profuse, maintain finger pressure over the wound while pushing immediately above and below the bleeding site. This will seal the areas where blood vessels enter the wound.

7 Get to an emergency room.

If you are being driven to the emergency room, recline with your head raised slightly. Keep firm pressure on the wound even if the bleeding seems to slow.

Be Aware

- If the blood flows in a steady stream, you have hit a vein and can block the blood flow by pressing above the wound. If the blood is spurting, you have lacerated an artery and can block the blood flow by pressing (hard) below the wound. (See step 6.)

- There are four jugular veins. The external jugulars, paired on the right and left sides of the neck, are vulnerable because they lie right under the surface of the skin. The internal jugulars, also paired, lie close to the center of the neck front, but are about an inch under the skin in a protective sheath. If you accidentally cut your neck razor-shaving and notice a great deal of bleeding, you've probably cut the external jugular.

HOW TO DEAL WITH BODY ODOR

1 Apply cologne or perfume.
If you are on the way to a date and discover a problem with body odor, find a drugstore or department store. Apply the scent liberally.

2 Change your shirt or remove the offending article of clothing.
A simple change of clothing can often eliminate the odor, especially from an undershirt. Purchase a new shirt if you have to.

3 In mid-date, use one of the following techniques in the bathroom:
- Wet a stack of paper towels with hot water and a bit of soap. Take a second stack of towels and wet them without adding soap. Wash under your arms and wherever necessary with the soapy towels, then rinse with the remaining towels.
- Obtain chamomile tea bags from your server if you are in a restaurant. Soak them in hot water, then wipe down the offending areas with the bags. If possible, leave them in place for several minutes.
- Obtain a handful of fresh rosemary from the kitchen, wet it slightly, and rub it over the offending areas.
- Apply bathroom soap (powdered works best) to the offending areas to mask the scent.

Soak chamomile teabags in hot water. Wipe the offending areas with the tea bags. If possible, leave the bags in place for several minutes.

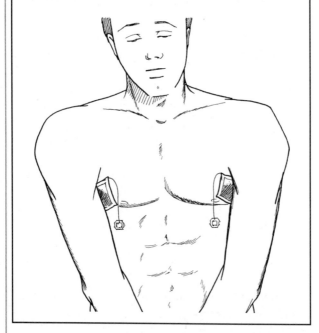

Be Aware

- To avoid B.O., try bathing using an antibacterial soap. Prolonged use can cause dryness, however.
- Avoid spicy or garlicky foods—these can cause body odor to worsen.
- Unusual body odor—not the typical "sweaty" smell—may indicate a more serious condition.
- Watch for the warning smells of B.O.:
  - Beer smell may indicate a yeast infection.
  - Nail polish smell may indicate diabetes.
  - Ammonia smell may indicate liver disease.

HOW TO DEAL WITH BAD BREATH

1 Chew gum or mints.

Excuse yourself from the table and head for the host's desk, where there may be a dish of mints. A waiter or busboy may also be able to give you a piece of gum. Go to the restroom and chew the gum for two minutes, then spit it out. This will get your saliva flowing and keep bad breath at bay for an hour or more. Chewing for more than a few minutes is not necessary. Sugar-free gum is best.

2 Chew parsley, mint, or a cinnamon stick.

On the way to the bathroom, pull your waiter aside and ask for one of these common garnishes. Parsley and fresh mint leaves are natural breath fresheners. A cinnamon stick, if chewed, will also clean your breath; do not use ground or powdered cinnamon. Most bartenders will have a stick on hand.

3 Order a salad or some fresh carrots.

If you cannot leave the table, order coarse foods that can help clean the tongue, a major source of bad breath.

Be Aware

• Food odors are generally not as bad as you think, but when possible, avoid onions and garlic during your date.

To freshen breath, chew on any of the following items:

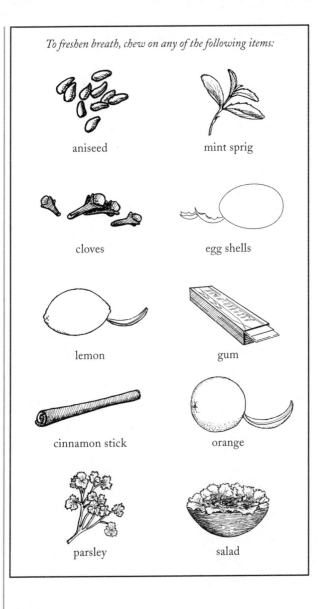

aniseed

mint sprig

cloves

egg shells

lemon

gum

cinnamon stick

orange

parsley

salad

How to Prevent Bad Breath

1 Floss.
Before going to bed, floss your teeth. Use unscented floss and smell it after each pass through. Areas that smell the worst need the most attention. Flossing may also help you live longer, as gum disease can shorten your life.

2 Sweep the tongue.
Gently sweep the mucus off the very back of your tongue with a commercially available tongue cleaner. Avoid cleaners made from sharp metal and do not scrape the tongue.

3 Brush with mouthwash.
Use an effective mouthwash. Shake if necessary, then pour some into the cap. Dip your toothbrush into it and brush your teeth properly for a few minutes. Do not use mouthwash and toothpaste at the same time as they can cancel out each other's active ingredients. Rinse and gargle with the rest of the mouthwash in the cap.

HOW TO OPEN A BOTTLE WITHOUT AN OPENER

ANOTHER BOTTLE

1 Hold the bottle you wish to open upright in your nondominant hand.

Grip the neck of the target bottle, placing your index finger over the back edge of the cap.

2 Hold the second bottle horizontally around the label.

Grip this bottle, the opener, as though shaking hands with the bottle.

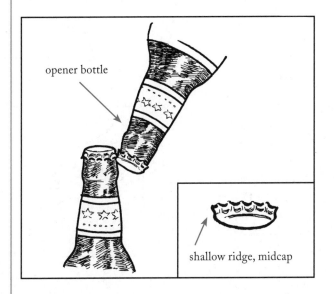

opener bottle

shallow ridge, midcap

3 Fit the shallow ridge found at midcap of the opener bottle under the bottom edge of the cap of the bottle you wish to open.

By using this ridge, and not the bottom of the cap, you will not risk opening the second bottle in step 4.

4 Using the opener bottle as a lever, press down and pry the cap off the target beer bottle.

5 Enjoy.

Alternate Method:
Hold both bottles end to end perpendicular to the ground, with the crimped edges of the caps together, locking them in place. Pull. Be careful, however, as either or both bottle caps could come off.

LIGHTER

1 Grip the bottle in your non-dominant hand.

Make a fist around the top of the bottle so that your thumb overlaps your index finger and the web between your thumb and index finger sits in the groove under the cap.

2 Fit the bottom of the lighter under the teeth of the cap.
Position the lighter so that it rests on the middle knuckle of your index finger.

3 Press the top of the lighter down and toward the bottle.
Use the index finger on your dominant hand to provide resistance.

4 Pry off the cap.
If necessary, turn the bottle and repeat.

TABLE EDGE

1 Put the teeth of the bottle cap against the edge of a table.
The cap should be on top of the table edge; the bottle should be below the table. Do not attempt on a soft wood or antique table.

2 Use your fist to hit the bottle.
The bottle will take a downward trajectory, and the cap will pop off.

SCREWDRIVER, SPOON, FORK, OR KNIFE

1 Place the implement under the bottle cap, as high as it will go.

2 Pry off the cap.
Slowly go around the cap and lift up each crimped area with the tool, similar to opening a can of paint.

3 When the cap starts to move, fit the tool higher up under the cap and remove it.

BELT BUCKLE

1 Unfasten your belt buckle. If your pants are in danger of falling down, sit.

2 Pull the "tooth" of the buckle to one side.

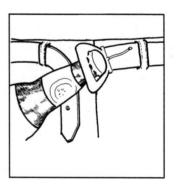

3 Fit the cap into the buckle so that one edge is wedged against the buckle.

4 Pry off.
Pull the bottle slowly. A quick tug may result in a spill.

5 Refasten your belt.

Deadbolt Lock

1 Fit your bottle into the lock.
Place the head of the bottle into
the recession in a doorframe into
which a deadbolt slips, so that
the cap fits against the notch in
the lock's frame.

2 Pull up slowly.
The bottle cap should pop right
off.

Fire Hydrant

1 Look for an arrow on top of the hydrant labeled
"open."

2 At the end of the arrow, locate
the recess between the screw
and the nut.

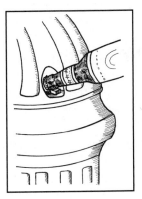

3 Insert the cap into the recess.

4 Press down slowly on the bottle
until the cap comes off.

In-Line Skate

1 | Place the cap between the shoe and the blade.
Hold on to the bottle with your dominant hand. If you are wearing the skate, use the hand opposite the skate to open the bottle.

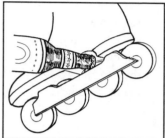

2 | Pull up slowly on the bottle and pry off.
Quickly right the bottle to avoid spilling.

Metal Pool Bridge

1 | Hold the stick of the bridge in one hand and a beer bottle in the other.
Do not attempt to open over the pool table.

2 | Position the cap inside the opening of the bridge.
Fit the cap snugly against the edge.

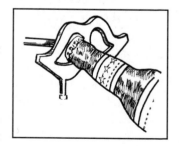

3 | Press down on the bottle. Slowly increase the pressure until the cap loosens. Right the bottle immediately to prevent spillage.

Vending Machine

1 Locate a newspaper, snack, or soda vending machine.
An older soda machine might actually have a bottle opener.

2 Place the cap in the coin return.
Wedge the cap against the top of the opening.

3 Press down slowly until the cap is removed.

Be Aware
• Never drink from a bottle with broken or chipped glass.

HOW TO GET YOUR DOG TO LIKE YOUR SIGNIFICANT OTHER

1   Introduce the canine to your significant other on neutral ground.

Coordinate the first meeting at a public place, such as a nearby park. Avoid introducing the two on the dog's home turf, which risks encouraging the dog to defend his territory around a stranger.

2   Instruct your significant other to approach the dog calmly.

This is particularly important if your pet is overly fearful or very dominant. Advise your companion to avoid prolonged eye contact (which can be construed as a threat) or immediately and enthusiastically petting the canine (which the dog might find unnerving). Coach your partner to greet the animal in a low-key manner. Later, if the dog seems amenable, your significant other can offer a pat on the back. Do not overdo it.

3   Provide treats.

Praise your dog for good behavior and offer him a treat. Even better, have your significant other offer him a treat.

Wear an article of your partner's clothing to familiarize the canine with her scent.

4 Wear a garment that has been in contact with your new companion.

When alone with your dog, wear an article of your partner's clothing. This will help familiarize the canine with your significant other's scent, making your dog more at ease when he actually encounters your significant other.

5 | Have your significant other feed the dog.
Occasionally a canine may develop dominance issues with a newcomer. To diffuse this, have your new friend feed the dog for a while. Being in charge of the animal's sustenance will make the person seem "dominant" in the eyes of your pet.

Be Aware

- A "significant other" might be a lover, a new roommate, or a newborn baby. Most of these steps also apply to introducing another dog, cat, or llama.
- If your dog's suspicion and distrust of a new acquaintance seems unshakable, do not dismiss it. Canines are experts at "reading" human personalities and intentions. He may understand your new friend's true nature far better than you do.

HOW TO DISGUISE YOURSELF AS A MEMBER OF THE OPPOSITE SEX

How To Disguise Yourself As a Man

⭐ Shower off perfume.
Scrub off any perfumes or feminine soap smells. Spray on some cologne or male deodorant after drying off.

⭐ Cut your hair.
Shape your hair into a short, masculine style. Cover with a baseball cap or other men's hat.

⭐ Simulate a beard.
Spread burnt cork lightly across your face to help give you a stubbled look.

⭐ Flatten your chest.
Put on a sports bra or tight T-shirt, then wrap a long bandage around your torso several times, starting at the top of your chest and moving downward to push your breasts down. Cover with another T-shirt.

⭐ Rough up your hands.
Rub your hands with dirt. Trim your nails and remove all nail polish, even clear polish.

✪ Sit with legs apart.
Do not cross your legs while sitting. With your feet flat on the ground, leave your knees slightly apart. Alternatively, rest one ankle on the opposite knee. Before going out, practice walking like a man in front of a mirror while wearing men's boots.

✪ Cover your neck and arms.
Unlike women, most men have a protruding Adam's apple and coarse forearm hair. Wear a high collar, long-sleeved shirt, or hooded sweatshirt.

✪ Wear oversized clothes.
Bulky shirts, jeans, sweatpants, or other pants with large pockets will hide your contours.

✪ Lower your voice.
Bring your voice up from deep in your diaphragm. Do not talk about your feelings. Keep your answers short.

✪ Look people in the eye.
Stare directly at people when you are talking to them. This will make it seem like you have nothing to hide and keep them from scrutinizing you for too long.

✪ Add a feminine scent.
Clean yourself thoroughly in a bath with a feminine soap, then lightly scent yourself with a quality brand of perfume.

✪ Remove all facial hair.
Shave off all the hair on your neck and face, then shave it again, getting as close as you can to your skin to eliminate all the stubble. Get rid of sideburns. Apply lotion to your face to make your skin moist.

✪ Pluck your eyebrows.
Get rid of stray hairs and try to achieve a thin, arched brow.

✪ Apply makeup.
Apply a tasteful amount of eyeliner, lipstick, and blush. Avoid foundation covering unless you absolutely need it to cover up stubborn beard stubble—and make sure it matches your natural skin tone. While some makeup will make you look like a woman, too much will make you look like a drag queen.

✪ Fix your hair.
If your hair is long enough, shape it into a typical feminine hairstyle. If your hair is relatively short, use a wig, but only a high-quality one. An ill-fitting wig made of cheap, synthetic material will draw more attention and scrutiny than short hair. If you can't find a good wig,

wear a headscarf or a hat with a floppy brim to help cover your face.

✪ Cover your neck.
Use a scarf or turtleneck. Most women, unlike most men, do not have protruding Adam's apples.

✪ Manicure your nails.
Thoroughly wash your hands, removing any dirt underneath the nails. Trim and shape your nails and cover them with a colored polish. Wear a pair of feminine gloves if your hands are hairy or scarred. If your arms are on the hairier side, shave them or wear a long-sleeved shirt.

✪ Walk with a wiggle.
Swivel your hips and your shoulders more when you walk. Put more weight on the front instead of the back of your feet. Practice walking in front of a mirror while wearing a good pair of women's shoes.

✪ Pick out your wardrobe.
Dress to blend in with the other women who will be in your vicinity. Select a dress or outfit that de-emphasizes your biceps, shoulders, and midsection. Add a little padding to approximate feminine curves in the hips, chest, and buttocks. Wear a woman's coat, if weather permits.

★ Carry a purse.
Put money and other small items you'll need for your escape into a purse. Add lipstick, a hairbrush, and perfume. Use a purse without a strap so you hold your hands in front of you—a more feminine position than dangling at your sides.

★ Cross your legs.
When sitting, place one knee over the top of the other.

★ Raise the pitch of your voice.
Close off your throat when you speak so you don't breathe from the diaphragm. Keep your answers short.

CHAPTER 3

ON THE DATE

HOW TO GET AN EMERGENCY RESERVATION

BRIBE

1 Determine how much to offer the maitre d' as a bribe.
The right amount will depend on the exclusivity and reputation of the establishment. Offer a minimum of $10. You usually get only one chance to try the bribe.

2 Fold the bill into your right palm.
Hold it between your thumb and forefinger.

3 Pass the bribe.
Shake his hand as you tell him how you are sure that he understands how important this night is to you. Be prepared, however, for the occasional maitre d' who takes your money and does not honor your request.

SOB STORY

1 Talk calmly to the maitre d'.
Controlled pleading can prove effective if you bend the right ear at the right time. A friendly, familiar demeanor is most likely to get the first available table. A whiny or arrogant voice will not help at all. If the maitre d' looks harried, wait until he or she has a moment to focus on you.

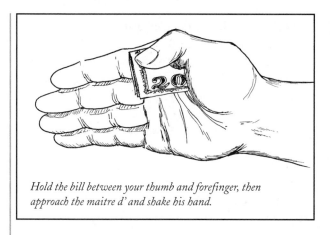

Hold the bill between your thumb and forefinger, then approach the maitre d' and shake his hand.

2 Explain your situation.
Be sure to stress the importance of the evening and the special need for a table, embellishing the facts as necessary: an anniversary dinner, a plan to propose marriage (but be prepared to produce a ring), a recovery from a long illness, an overdue reunion.

3 Speak with emotion.
Catch your voice, have difficulty breathing, shed a tear. You become harder to ignore. Also, the maitre d' will not want you upsetting the other waiting guests and creating a scene.

4 Appeal to the host's understanding nature.
Create the impression that you would be especially embarrassed in front of your date, since you told her you had a reservation.

5 | Look to fellow diners for sympathy.
If you cannot sway the host or maitre d', approach other diners and bribe or persuade them into giving up their table. Use the special event strategy (step 2, above). However, be careful to avoid offending the patrons or embarrassing your date. It is best to try this when your date leaves your side for a moment.

6 | Pull rank.
Your final option is to play the "do you know who I am?" card. Unfortunately, you actually have to be somebody for this one to work.

Be Aware
- Do not try the "lost reservation" ploy; no one believes it anyway. Claiming that the restaurant is at fault for misplacing your reservation provokes confrontation rather than conciliation, and rarely results in a table.
- You can try the "celebrity name drop," but it could backfire. Asking for a table in the name of a celebrity will sometimes get you seated even though the celebrity is "late" in arriving, but the host may also ask you to wait until your group is all present before seating you—and you will be precluded from using other tactics.

HOW TO SAVE YOUR DATE FROM CHOKING

1 Speak firmly.
Keep your voice low and your sentences short. All communications should be in the imperative. Explain that you are going to perform the Heimlich maneuver.

2 Tell your date to stand up and stay put.

3 Hug your date from behind.
Put your arms around your date and make one hand into a fist.

4 Place your fist in your date's solar plexus.
The solar plexus is the first soft spot in the center of the body, between the navel and the ribs.

5 Place your other hand, palm open, over your fist.

6 Tell your date to bend forward slightly.
If your date does not respond, push on the upper back and repeat, "Lean forward."

7 Pull your fist in and up.
Use force and a quick motion. This will push out the residual lung gas under pressure, clearing any obstructions from the trachea.

8 Repeat steps 3 through 7 several times if choking persists.

9 After several unsuccessful attempts, instruct your date to bend over the back of a chair.
The top of the chair should be at the level of your date's hips.

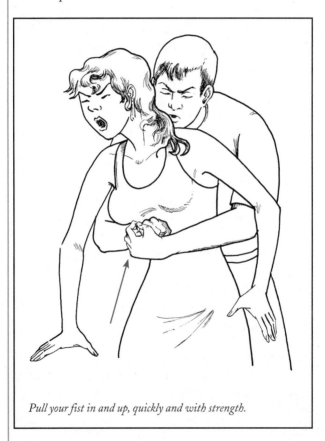

Pull your fist in and up, quickly and with strength.

10 Strike your date between the shoulder blades with the heel of your open hand.

The blow generates gaseous pressure in a blocked airway and, with a head-down position, sometimes works when the Heimlich does not.

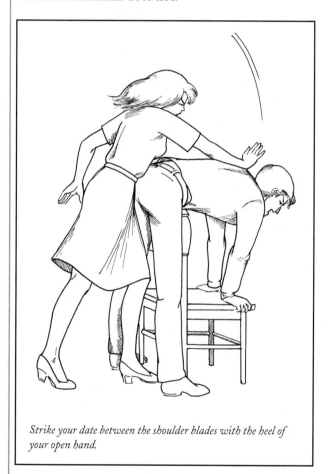

Strike your date between the shoulder blades with the heel of your open hand.

Be Aware

- If the choking is noiseless—or if your date raises her hands to her throat—then the air passage may be completely blocked and you must proceed quickly.
- If your date is coughing or gagging, you simply need to be polite, smile sympathetically, and offer water when the choking is over. Water does nothing for choking, but it gives the choker some time to regain dignity.
- In most cases, the first thrust of the Heimlich maneuver will dislodge the choked item from the trachea. Once the choking is over, your date will need some time to recover: a sip of brandy, a quiet moment. Do not rush your date to the emergency room; in most cases, there is no need to go to the hospital after the blockage has been removed.

HOW TO SURVIVE
IF YOU HAVE
EXCESSIVE GAS

1 Limit your lactose intake during the date.
Many people suffer from an inability to digest milk sugar, or lactose. Colon bacteria ferment the milk sugar, forming a gas that creates a bloated feeling. Keep your intake to less than half a cup at a sitting, and avoid dairy products before your date.

2 Eat a small meal.
Eating a huge dinner on a date is a sure-fire way to precipitate gas.

3 Avoid gas-forming foods.
Bacteria ferment the indigestible carbohydrates in beans, broccoli, cabbage, and other vegetables and fruits into gases.

4 Drink peppermint tea.
Replace an after-dinner drink with a cup or two of peppermint tea. This herb may give you some relief from the gas discomfort that follows a meal.

5 Emit the gas in private.
As a last resort, head to the bathroom. If you feel bloated but are unable to pass gas easily, you can facilitate the emission of gas as follows:

Kneel on the floor, bend forward, and stretch your arms out in front of you. Keep your buttocks high in the air, forming a triangle with your upper body and the floor.

Place paper towels on the floor. Kneel on the towels, bend forward to the floor, and stretch your arms out in front of you. Keep your buttocks high in the air, forming a triangle with your upper body and the floor. This position will force out the unwanted gas and relieve the pressure.

Be Aware

- On average, humans produce 3/4 of a liter of gas daily, which is released 11 to 14 times a day.
- Men typically produce more gas than women because they consume more food.

GASSY FOODS TO AVOID

No two digestive systems are alike. Experiment with foods to determine which ones affect you most. In the meantime, exercise caution around the following high-risk items:

- Beans (particularly baked beans)
- Borscht
- Broccoli
- Brussels sprouts
- Cabbage
- Carbonated beverages
- Cauliflower
- Chili
- Cucumbers
- Fatty foods
- Fresh fruit
- Grains and fiber, especially pumpernickel bread
- Gum
- Onions
- Oysters
- Salads (green)

HOW TO SURVIVE IF YOUR CREDIT CARD IS DECLINED

Talk with the Manager

1 Be subtle.

After the waiter informs you that your card has been declined, excuse yourself from the table and head for the reception desk. Explain the situation to the manager and show whatever identification you have. Ask him or her what you might do. Call the credit card company and inquire about your card. Speak firmly and sternly to the company. Ask the credit card company to extend your credit temporarily and immediately by the amount that you need.

2 Offer collateral.

Offer to leave something of value until you can return with the payment. Do not use your date as collateral. Offer a watch or a driver's license.

3 Provide references.

If you are known at any other restaurants, ask the manager to check with them, and say the management there will vouch for you. Promise to return immediately with payment.

4 Seek funds.

Order another drink for your date (at the table or the bar) and confess the situation. Dash home for money or to a friend's house for a loan. Alternatively—unless it is the first date—you can ask your date to pay.

DINE AND DASH

1 Accept the consequences.

You will never be able to be seen in this restaurant again if you skip out. Your date may be offended and embarrassed. And if this restaurant is in an area that you frequent, you may be identified and caught later.

2 Tell your date the plan.

You do not want to catch your date off guard. Do not abandon your date, since she will likely be very upset and may help the authorities track you down. Plan to leave together.

3 Plan your route of escape.

The best route is through the front door. However, restaurant staff may give chase. Assume that you will be followed. Visualize where you are going once you exit the restaurant. Head toward crowded or darkened areas.

4 Wait until the staff is busy.

Have your belongings within reach for a hasty retreat. Do not appear anxious or ready to bolt.

5 | Pretend to pay the bill with cash.
Place whatever bills you have in the bill holder with the check. The illusion of a cash payment will buy you valuable minutes of escape time; your waiter isn't likely to count the money until he reaches the nearest available cash register.

6 | Walk confidently out the door.
Proceed slowly and with authority.

7 | As soon as you are outside, run.

8 | If you are being followed, do not go directly to your car.
It is very easy for your pursuer to jot down your license number. Wait at least twenty minutes before returning to your vehicle.

Be Aware

- Stiffing the restaurant is illegal and may land you in jail, where the food is not very good. Arrange to pay the restaurant, directly or through a third party, as soon as you can. Include a message encouraging them to be more understanding of customers with credit card problems in the future.

Wash Dishes

1 Offer to wash dishes.
Tell the manager that you are willing to work to cover the cost of your meal. Explain that you have experience with the technology involved.

2 Prepare to get wet.
Take off your jacket, your watch, and any jewelry. (Men should also remove tie and long-sleeve shirt, if wearing an undershirt.) Take off your glasses (unless you have a major problem seeing without them.) It is hot and wet in the kitchen. Ask for an apron, if available.

To save time, ask your date to pre-rinse the dirty dishware while you slide the loaded racks into the dishwasher.

3 Pre-rinse the dirty dishware.

Remove the dirty dishes from the bus tub. Load the dishes into a square peg rack (a 20-by-20-inch plastic tray with holes in the bottom), place the peg rack over a slop sink, and rinse with a hose.

4 Lift the door to the dishwasher and slide in the rack.

5 Close the dishwasher door and begin the wash cycle. Most machines begin automatically when locked, but you may need to press the start button. When the cycle is done, raise the door on the opposite side of the machine and remove the peg rack. Some systems utilize a conveyor belt that has claws to grab onto and pull the peg rack through the wash cycle.

6 Place the peg rack with the clean dishes in a drying rack.

The drying rack may be a wheeled racking system that holds many peg racks. Or it could be a slanted rack mounted on the wall. When the rack is placed on the angled wall unit, the excess water drips onto the stainless steel shelving. The dishes are now ready for use.

HOW TO FEND OFF COMPETITORS FOR YOUR DATE

1 Evaluate the situation.
Are you on a first date that is not going well? Is your date paying more attention to the interloper than to you? Do you want to continue dating this person?

2 Determine the seriousness of the offense.
Is it a passing rude drunk, a persistent boor, or someone seriously interested in leaving with your date? How big is the interloper? These factors will determine your response.

3 Stand your ground.
Put your arms around your date, whisper in her ear, and kiss and caress her. Show the suitor that your date is enamored with you, and you with her.

4 Place yourself in the "pickup screen" position.
Wedge yourself between the suitor and your date, with your back to the suitor. Try to block the suitor's path of vision. An "accidental" bump or push with your shoulders or buttocks may be appropriate.

Assume the "pickup screen" position by wedging yourself between the suitor and your date, with your back to the suitor. Try to block the suitor's path of vision.

5 Ask the interloper to stop.
Politely but firmly explain that you are trying to have a conversation with your date and that you would both prefer to be left alone. If the suitor persists, use humor or sarcasm to diffuse the situation. Tell him you can offer him a few phone numbers, or tell him that tonight she's taken, but you will let him know when she's available.

6 If the suitor is with friends, enlist their help to rein him in.

7 Ask your date to tell the suitor to back off.
Your date should tell him that she's flattered but not interested.

8 Try to leave.
If given the choice, choose flight over fight. Suggest to your date that you both move to a table or go to a new establishment. A fight generally doesn't make the evening go any better.

How to Treat a Black Eye

1 Make a cold compress.
Put crushed ice in a plastic bag and wrap the bag in a thin piece of cloth. Alternatively, use a bag of frozen vegetables or a cold, raw steak.

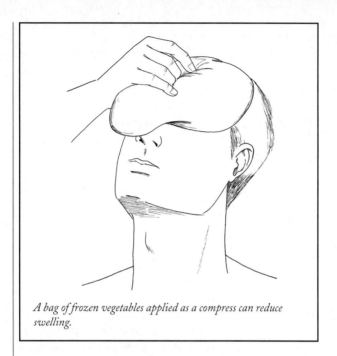

A bag of frozen vegetables applied as a compress can reduce swelling.

2 Sit down, tilt your head back, and cover your eye with the compress.

Use minimal pressure. This position allows gravity to aid in swelling reduction. If the compress is too cold to hold over your eye, use a thicker cloth. Keep the compress over your eye for an hour.

3 Take a painkiller.

For pain, take acetaminophen or ibuprofen.

How to Treat a Broken Nose

1 | Stop the bleeding.
Tilt your head back slightly. Pinch the bridge of your nose (the region just below the hard cartilage) closed, not just the nostrils. Hold a tissue underneath your nostrils to catch the blood.

2 | Apply a cold pack or ice immediately.
Keep your head tilted back. Continue to apply ice as needed to keep the swelling down.

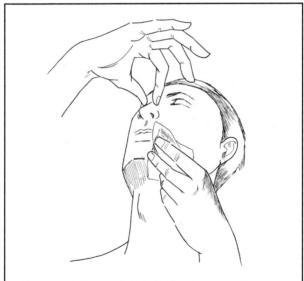

If your nose is broken, pinch the bridge of your nose (the region just below the hard cartilage) closed, not the nostrils. Hold a tissue underneath your nostrils to catch the blood.

3 Do not reset a broken nose yourself.

The only reason for you to attempt to relocate the position of the nose is if you are having trouble breathing through your mouth. If you aren't getting any air, you can attempt to adjust the position of your nose so that you can breathe through it, but this will be quite painful.

4 Seek medical attention.

Be Aware

The following symptoms indicate a more serious injury and the immediate need for professional care:

- Bleeding from the nose does not stop within 10 minutes
- Bleeding from both nostrils
- Trouble breathing through your nose
- Eye pain, trouble seeing, or blood on the surface of the eye
- Clear, watery fluid leaking out of the nose after the injury
- Swelling, bruising, or tenderness extending over the cheek area or below the eye

HOW TO DEAL WITH A DRUNKEN DATE

1   Avoid confrontation.
You realize your date is drunk, but he might not believe
it. Keep the conversation light and happy, but don't let
him have any more to drink. Suggest a change of plans,
like a walk outside.

2   Keep your date on his feet.
Support him as needed. Put your arm around his waist,
putting his arm over your shoulder. If that doesn't
work, try holding him up by the belt. If you cannot
hold your date upright, keep him seated and call a taxi.

3   Lead your date out into the air.
Bars are often smoky and short of oxygen, and oxygen
is a major factor in reducing drunkenness. Calmly walk
your date outside to get some fresh air into his lungs.
This may help him become more awake and aware. If
he objects, say you need to go outside to make a phone
call.

4   Encourage your date to vomit.
If your date is so drunk that he cannot walk, or if he is
speaking unintelligibly, he should expel alcohol from
his system. Vomiting purges the stomach and prevents
more alcohol from entering the bloodstream. Make
sure your date rehydrates after purging. If your date

Suggest a walk outside to get some fresh air.

falls to the floor and passes out, roll him onto his side to prevent him from choking on his vomit.

5 Watch for alcohol poisoning.
Signs of alcohol poisoning include tremors, unresponsiveness, unconsciousness, and lack of breathing. If

you suspect alcohol poisoning, position your date on his side, stay with him, and have someone call 911 for assistance.

6 Help your date to sober up.
See the next section, "How to Sober Up Fast."

Be Aware

- Common "cures" for drunkenness such as coffee or a cold shower are generally not effective; they will simply produce a more awake or wet drunk.

- Your body burns off approximately one drink an hour. It makes little difference if your drink is a 1-ounce shot of whiskey, a 5-ounce glass of wine, or a 12-ounce mug of beer—all contain similar amounts of alcohol. If you consume more than one drink per hour, you run the risk of becoming intoxicated. To minimize dehydration, drink a glass of water between rounds.

- If your drunk date goes to the restroom, stand outside and keep talking to him to be sure he remains conscious and responsive.

HOW TO DEAL WITH "THE SPINS"

1 Focus your gaze on a stationary object in the room. Keep your eyes open. Avoid looking at ceiling fans. Stare at the object for one minute.

2 Close your eyes.

3 Picture the object you were looking at. Imagine that the object is imprinted on the inside of your eyelids.

4 Open your eyes. If the spinning returns, stare at your object for one minute.

5 Close your eyes. Repeat steps 3 and 4.

6 Repeat steps 3, 4, and 5 until the spinning stops or you pass out.

Be Aware
* The spins usually occur when your eyes are closed. Watch television, go out for some air, or eat a meal—anything to stay awake and keep your eyes open until you sober up.

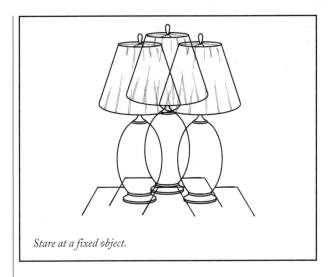

Stare at a fixed object.

- Eating reduces drinking-related sickness by reducing the speed at which alcohol in the stomach is absorbed into the bloodstream. Eat before drinking: Once you have the spins, it is too late.
- Alcohol is a diuretic and dehydrates. After drinking, replace lost fluid, vitamins, and electrolytes by consuming sports drinks. Avoid drinking excessive amounts of plain water, which will dilute the sodium concentration in the body.

How to Vomit Correctly

1 Be prepared.
Vomiting may be preceded by sweating, nausea, gagging, increased saliva, or the sensation of swelling under the tongue.

2 | Move quickly.
Get to a quiet bathroom or a private area with an appropriate receptacle, such as a toilet, trash can, or metal bowl. If outdoors, look for an area secluded by trees or bushes. Avoid public spaces.

3 | Remove necktie or necklace.

4 | Open collar.
Unbutton your shirt at least two buttons and pull the sides apart. If you are wearing a pullover, remove it completely, if time permits. Tie back long hair.

5 | Relax.
Do not resist.

6 | Target a destination.
Vomit into the receptacle. If vomiting into a toilet, grip the sides for support.

7 | Wait.
The first bout of vomiting may not be the last. Wait several minutes to make sure you remain in control.

8 | Clean up.
Wash your hands and face, rinse out your mouth, and brush your teeth.

9 | Return to the party.

HOW TO SOBER UP FAST

1 | Avoid pills.
Do not take ibuprofen, acetaminophen, or aspirin just before, during, or after drinking. Acetaminophen may cause liver damage in conjunction with alcohol. Ibuprofen can cause severe stomach irritation. Aspirin thins the blood, which may exacerbate a hangover.

2 | Drink lots of fluids.
Dehydration from alcohol can be treated with water, sweet juices, or sports drinks. Orange juice and tomato juice contain potassium, which will help overcome the shaky feeling of a major hangover.

3 | Take vitamins.
A good multivitamin or vitamin B complex combats vitamin depletion.

4 | Eat.
Starchy foods—bread, crackers, rice, or pasta—break down into sugar, which speeds absorption of alcohol into your system. A spoonful of honey (which is high in fructose) helps to quickly burn off any remaining alcohol in the stomach. Listen to your body's cravings: if eggs sound good, eat them. If something spicy sounds better, eat that. There are no right or wrong things to eat; just take your food slowly and in small amounts.

5 Rest or sleep for as long as possible.
Repeat steps 2 through 5 if you wake up with a hangover.

How to Prevent a Hangover

- Eat before you begin to drink and snack while drinking.
- If you do not eat, coat your stomach with a full glass of milk.
- Pace yourself and drink water between drinks.
- Drink clear liquors. Some spirits are higher in congeners (impurities) than others; red wine, brandies (including cognac), and whiskies usually have more than other types of alcohol. Generally, the clearer your spirit, the fewer impurities and the less severe the hangover.
- Champagne and mixed drinks made with carbonated sodas allow for faster alcohol absorption; they should be sipped slowly.
- Know your limits. In most states, a Blood Alcohol Content (B.A.C.) of .10 means you are legally drunk—and some states now use the stricter .08 B.A.C. For most average-size adults, this can mean as few as two drinks in an hour.
- Do not mix your liquors. Each spirit has different toxins that must be processed by your liver. It is best not to overload it.
- Before going to bed, have a snack of a banana or cheese and crackers.
- Keep water beside your bed and drink it if you awaken during the night.

HOW TO CARRY A DATE WHO IS PASSED OUT

1 Plan to carry your date only for a short distance.
Your destination should be a nearby couch, taxi, or bed. Do not attempt to carry him a long way.

2 Prepare to lift.
Bend your knees and place your stronger arm under your date's back and the other under his knees. Your arms should go all the way under and across his body.

3 Begin to lift your date.
Use the strength of your legs and knees, holding them close to your body and keeping your back straight. Do not lift with your back.

4 Stand up quickly.
In one continuous motion, rotate your date's body so that your stronger arm guides him over your opposite shoulder. The motion should be like tossing a sack of potatoes. His upper body should be hanging over your back, his lower body hanging over your front. Steady him with your other hand.

5 Walk to your destination.

Place your stronger arm under your date's back.

Keep your back straight and lift with your knees.

Rotate your date's body over your opposite shoulder. The motion should be like tossing a sack of potatoes.

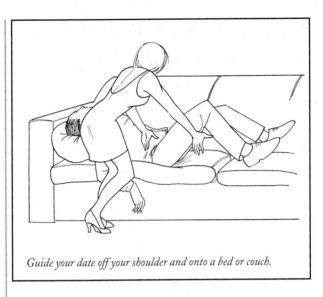

Guide your date off your shoulder and onto a bed or couch.

6 Lower your date.
Bending your knees and keeping your back straight, guide your date off your shoulder and onto a bed or couch or into a chair.

HOW TO SURVIVE IF YOU ARE STOPPED BY THE POLICE

1 Pull over immediately.

Put your hazard lights on, take off your sunglasses, turn off the radio, and turn off the engine. Roll down your window. Keep your hands in plain sight, preferably on the steering wheel. Make sure your date's hands are also in view.

Address the officer as "Officer." Respect for authority will get you out of the situation much more quickly and easily.

2 | Address the officer as "Officer."
Displaying proper respect will get you out of the situation much more quickly and easily.

3 | Always tell the truth about your record.
The police officer already knows (or will soon know) the answers to the questions asked. Do not claim that you have a clean driving record if this is not the case.

4 | Do not argue with or challenge the officer.
Not only will you look foolish and/or arrogant in front of your date, your comments may be recorded on the officer's copy of the ticket so they can be used to refresh the officer's memory in court. Do not give the officer a reason to take a personal interest in you or your case, which would only encourage the officer to show up in court if you decide to fight the ticket. (Many defendants succeed in court because the officer is not present to testify.)

5 | Do not falsely claim your innocence.
The officer has seen you do it, and denying the infraction or making lame excuses will only serve to irritate the officer.

6 | Use the presence of your date to help you.
Try saying, "Officer, I'm sorry. I'm on a date and I guess I was pretty distracted. I'm a bit nervous and probably was paying more attention to her than to my driving. I'll be more careful." This may appeal to the officer's sense of romance, helping you get off completely.

IF YOU ARE ARRESTED

1 Contact a bail bondsman.

A bondsman will need to know the name of the jail you are in, the charges against you, the amount of your bail, and your booking number. The bondsman will charge you a fee of about 10 percent of your total bail amount and then make a guarantee to the court on your behalf that you will show up for your court date. (If bail is set at $50,000, for example, you will be required to pay the bondsman a nonrefundable fee of approximately $5,000.)

2 Be prepared to put up collateral.

When a bondsman writes a bail bond for you, he is on the hook for the entire amount of your bail should you not show up in court. He will demand a guarantee that you can pay him the full amount if you should jump bail. Ninety percent of the time, large bail bonds are secured with real property. Evaluate your assets in light of the amount of bail.

HOW TO WIN A BAR BET

Make bets that you know you will win, or perform a surefire bar trick for drinks. Select a mark, preferably someone who has been drinking heavily.

Brandy Snifter and Cherry

You will need a small brandy snifter, an empty glass, and a stemless maraschino cherry.

1 Place the snifter upside down over the cherry.

2 Wager a free drink that you can get the cherry into the empty glass without touching the cherry or empty glass.
The cherry can touch only the snifter, which must remain upside down. Squashing the cherry onto the rim is prohibited.

3 Use centrifugal force.
When he bets, show him the power of centrifugal force. Hold the base of the snifter and rotate it quickly on the bar top. When the cherry starts spinning inside the glass, lift the snifter off the table. Keep rotating the snifter and hold it over the glass. When you slow your rotation, the cherry will drop into the glass. Collect your free drink.

Rotate snifter.

Lift snifter off the table as the cherry spins.

Drop the cherry into the target glass.

A Race to the Finish

1 Identify your mark.
At the bar, find a small group of men drinking together who seem tipsy, but not so drunk that they will try to kill you when played for fools.

2 Make your proposition.
Sit down next to the group, and casually say "You guys want to see something cool?" State the proposed bet simply and clearly: "Anyone want to bet I can drink three beers before you can drink a single shot?"

3 Let them decide who will take the bet.
Faced with a challenge, a group of men will naturally jockey for supremacy by mocking or goading each other into taking the bet.

4 Let the mark determine the stakes.
Allow the other person to set the stakes, especially if his friends are suggesting he will lose. Offer gentle reassurance such as, "It's totally up to you. Whatever you want to make it." And then whatever he proposes, up the ante by saying, "Oh, okay. Or we could make it a real bet. Whatever you want."

5 State the rules.
Clearly say what the bet is and how it works. "I will drink three beers before you drink a single shot. You give me a one-beer head start, and neither of us can touch the other's glasses.

6 | Hear it back.
Have the mark repeat the rules back to you, and make sure that all his friends and anyone else present can hear, so there are plenty of witnesses.

7 | Put the money on the bar.
Illustrate your commitment to the wager by suggesting that both you and the mark place your money directly on the bar in front of you. This will also allow you to collect the money more easily once you win.

8 | Feign second thoughts.
As the bartender brings the drinks, suddenly look anxious and say things such as, "Oh wait, did I get that right?" Try to back out: "You know what? Forget the whole thing." When the mark presses you, relent and agree to go through with it. He may try to raise the stakes of the wager; if so, reluctantly agree.

9 | Win the bet.
After you drink your head start beer, place the empty glass over his shot glass. This way he cannot drink his drink, because he's not allowed to touch your glass, per the rules of the bet. Finish your other two beers.

10 | Be gracious.
If the mark seems upset, offer to buy him a beer (with his own money) from the winnings on the bar. You've still come out several beers ahead.

HOW TO GET INTO AN EXCLUSIVE NIGHTCLUB

1   Wear expensive shoes.
Do not dress sloppily or outlandishly in an attempt to be "unique" or "interesting."

2   Go on a slow night.
Pick a night when fewer people will be trying to get in. In the summer, try a Friday or Saturday night. During all other seasons, go on a Monday, Tuesday, or Wednesday night. Avoid nightclubs during high-profile events such as Fashion Week (twice yearly) and the New York Film Festival (early fall).

3   Travel in a group.
Approach with no more than six people, including at least three women. The women should give no indications of being "taken," such as holding hands with the men in the group; holding hands with one another is okay.

4   Remain calm.
Maintain a laid-back, sober attitude while in line. Do not be argumentative with the doorman, the club staff, or with passersby. Do not name-drop or otherwise try to bluff the doorman into thinking you are more important or interesting than you are. Do not

Do not give anyone a "high five."

attempt to bribe the doorman or bouncer for entry. Do not complain when others arrive and get in while you are waiting. Do not bring a book to read while in line.

5 | Be casual when you do get in.

Nod calmly at the doorman as he waves you inside. Do not give anyone a "high five." Do not begin dancing until you are on the dance floor.

Be Aware

To increase your odds of being allowed in on a subsequent visit:

- Don't tell anyone you are from Jersey.
- Order full bottles rather than individual drinks. If there is a price for table service, or for use of a "VIP" area, pay it willingly. Tip at least 35 percent on each round of drinks and food; if possible, calculate the tip without reference to a calculator or wallet-sized tip card.
- If you see celebrities, do not ask for autographs or take photographs. Be polite but not overly flirtatious with the bar staff and cocktail waitresses.
- Tip the doorman at least $50 as you exit the club.

CHAPTER 4

GETTING IT ON

HOW TO DEAL WITH A BAD KISSER

Too Aggressive

⭐ Slow him down.
Ask your date to kiss more gently. Say, "Can I show you the way I really like to kiss?" and slowly lean forward to offer a demonstration.

⭐ Kiss your date.

⭐ Draw away from the kiss.
Briefly drawing away from the kiss is another way of saying slow down.

⭐ Gently hold his face.
Your hands can provide a caress, and also prevent him from zooming back in for more.

⭐ Tilt his head.
While your hands are in place, tilt his head to the angle of greatest comfort. Tilt your head accordingly.

⭐ Surround his mouth with gentler kisses.
Reinforce the message by sighing and saying, "I love it like this."

⭐ Repeat as necessary.

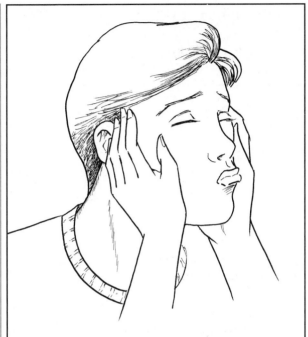

Tilt his head to the angle of greatest comfort, then adjust your position accordingly. Use your hands to hold him back or draw him in.

Be Aware

- Very aggressive tongue kissing may be just right when you are very aroused, but not so great when you are just beginning. Be careful not to scare him away from things you might enjoy later.

Too Passive

✪ Look your date in the eye.
A warm, smiling gaze signals affection and also lets him know something is about to happen.

✪ Hold his face.

✪ Kiss him passionately.
The kiss should be as deep and passionate as you want his to be. Remember to tilt your date's head before kissing him.

✪ Break away from the kiss.
Murmur, "Mmm, kiss me back harder." You are taking charge of the situation.

✪ Pause and redirect.
If you are still not getting the desired result—if his tongue is not responding—shift to lip-focused rather than deep-mouth kissing.

Be Aware
• You may be dealing with someone who thinks your kissing style is too aggressive. He may be passively resisting your technique instead of trying to slow you down by using the more direct response to "too aggressive" kissing (see above).

Too Wet

⭐ Keep your kisses focused on the lips.
Do not venture inside the mouth.

⭐ Use your thumbs to wipe away excess wetness.
Gently outline his lips with a thumb or other finger.
This will serve as a sensual caress and will also remove
excess moisture.

How to Deliver the Perfect Kiss

⭐ Cradle your date's face with your hands.
Look into his eyes.

⭐ Tilt his head.

⭐ Tilt your head.

⭐ Bring your mouth toward his mouth.
Gradually move closer.

⭐ Gently touch your lips to his.
Focus initially on the lips, giving soft, quick kisses.
Slowly part your lips, letting your tongue softly dart
out to touch his lips. This is an excellent way to gauge
your partner's receptiveness to furthering the kiss. If
lips part, proceed to the next level.

✪ Explore delicately with your tongue.
Open your mouth wider and push your tongue into his mouth. Probe the various parts of his mouth. Run your tongue over the teeth. Imagine your tongue fencing with your partner's tongue, lunging, darting, and parrying.

✪ Take frequent breaks.
Keeping your tongues inside each other's mouths for an extended period of time will produce a very sloppy, wet kiss. Move your head away from his every so often. This will also allow you to catch your breath.

✪ Know when to stop.
End the kiss before your jaw begins to ache, or before you are both worn out. It may be time to move on to other activities, or it may be fine to stop and leave him wanting more.

Be Aware
• If either or both of you wear glasses, remove them prior to a prolonged kissing session. Wearing glasses for a medium-intensity, brief kiss is acceptable, but glasses may hinder greater intimacy (and they may get fogged up or even scratched). Set them someplace safe, where you will not be likely to roll onto them later.

HOW TO REMOVE DIFFICULT CLOTHING

BACK-CLASPING BRA (WITH ONE HAND)

1 Move your date forward.
If your date is lying on her back or leaning against a sofa, you will not have the necessary space to attempt this maneuver. Use a gentle embrace to guide her into a position so that you have access to her back.

2 Visualize the clasp.
Most bras have a hook-and-eye closure. The hooks are generally on her right side; the eyes will be on her left side.

3 Reach your right hand around to the clasp.
Bend your index finger over the bra clasp and place it between the fabric and her skin.

4 Brace your thumb against the eyes of the clasp.

5 Holding your index finger down, push the hook-side of the bra with your thumb.
It may take a few attempts before you get good at this, so do not be discouraged—try again.

6 Slide the now-open bra off her arms.

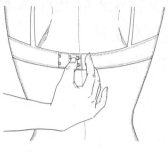

Brace your thumb against the eyes of the clasp.

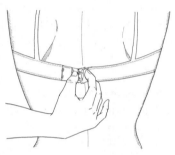

Holding your index finger down, push the hookside of the bra with your thumb.

Slide the now-open bra off her arms.

Be Aware

- The bigger the breasts, the bigger the challenge, since the closure on her bra is bearing more weight and is likely to be more taut.

FRONT-CLASPING BRA

✪ Determine the type of clasp.

There are two different varieties: a pin-in-slot clasp, which has a pin inserted vertically in a slot, and a clicker clasp. Clicker clasps, when closed, often look like a circle or an oval.

✪ For a pin-in-slot clasp, pull the pin upward.

This will free the two cups, and you can proceed to step 4.

✪ For a clicker clasp, push both ends away from you.

Place your thumbs at the center of the clasp and, using a motion similar to snapping a small wafer in half, apply pressure until it unclicks. Then lift up and separate the two halves of the closure. Depending on the clasp, you will need to raise either the left side or the right side first; try it one way, then the other.

✪ Slide the now-open bra off her arms.

Be Aware

- To maximize intimacy, maintain eye contact throughout the entire process. Do not look away unless you need to take a quick glance at the closure.

Pull firmly and steadily with your right hand. To avoid injuring the wearer, do not jerk the boot.

TIGHT BOOTS

⭐ Sprinkle powder down the shaft of each boot.
Talcum powder or baking powder will reduce the sweat and humidity inside the boots, making them easier to remove.

⭐ Position your date on the edge of a bed or couch.

✪ Position yourself opposite your date.
Sit in a chair braced against a wall, or rest one knee on the floor with the other foot flat on the floor.

✪ Cup the heel of the boot in your right hand.
Place your left hand on the area of the boot that covers the front of the leg/shin. Instruct your date to relax the foot in the boot.

✪ Pull firmly and steadily with your right hand.
You should feel some give in the heel. When you cannot move the boot anymore, gently rock the boot back and forth. Your date should point the foot only slightly. To avoid injuring the wearer, do not jerk the boot.

✪ Slide the boot off slowly.
Caress the newly released foot.

HOW TO FAKE AN ORGASM

1 Begin your vocal and physical ascent.
During sexual activity, start to make noise and move rhythmically.

2 Moan and cry out, building in volume and intensity.
You may say your partner's name over and over. Many people, in the thralls of ecstasy, will blurt out sentences or requests that are utterly incomprehensible: try this occasionally.

3 Move faster rhythmically and then increasingly "out of control."
As you approach "climax," increase the tempo of your movements, particularly of the hips. Add jerky movements. If you have not moved or vocalized much before you start to fake the orgasm, it will seem all the more fake, so you might need to fake enjoyment all the way through. (Note: If you do not usually move your hips during sex, try it. You may find it affects your arousal enough that you will need less faking.)

4 Contract your muscles.
For many people, this is an involuntary side effect of an orgasm; the classic examples are toe-curling or fingers clutching the sheets. You might also arch your back, scrunch your facial muscles, or open your mouth wide.

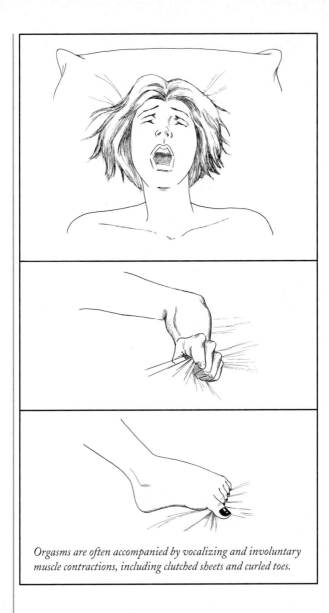

Orgasms are often accompanied by vocalizing and involuntary muscle contractions, including clutched sheets and curled toes.

5 Ratchet up the moaning and writhing in volume and intensity.

6 Culminate in a loud moan or cry.

7 Slow down immediately, tensing your body.

8 Relax, as if exhausted or spent.
Smile with enjoyment.

How to Detect a Real Orgasm

Real orgasms are not always as theatrical and loud as fake ones. Some people are silent comers and do not exhibit many visible signs. Real orgasms tend to have some or all of the following elements:
* Changes in breathing
* Increased vocalizations
* Intensified movements
* Involuntary muscle contractions
* A pink or reddish flush on the face and chest
* Sweat on the shoulders
* Pelvic muscle contractions

Be Aware

- Be sure that you want to fake the orgasm. You will be sending your partner a message that you are enjoying the sex more than you really are. If your partner is an ongoing lover or spouse, think hard before giving him or her the impression that he or she is doing everything right when that is not the case. If you are enjoying a one-night encounter, consider why it should make a difference to you if your partner thinks you have had an orgasm or not.

- Men can fake orgasms too, particularly if a condom is being used.

- Do not accuse your partner of faking an orgasm if they are not demonstrative, spasmodic, and loud. Conversely, do not accuse your partner of faking if they display all the characteristics of a faked orgasm.

HOW TO CREATE PRIVACY IF YOUR DOOR DOES NOT LOCK

BLOCKADE A DOOR THAT OPENS INWARD

1 Find a straight-backed wooden or metal chair.

2 Shut the door.

3 Place the chair about a foot from the door.
How far away you place it will depend upon how tall the chair's back is, so adjust the distance accordingly.

4 Tilt the chair backward so that the top of the chair is wedged underneath the doorknob.
The seat should be facing upward. If necessary, pull the bottom of the chair out a bit so that the top of the chair will fit under the knob.

5 Push down on the front of the seat or the bottom of the front legs.
When the chair is securely wedged, kick it in further to make the blockade tight.

6 Place a large item of furniture (a trunk or dresser) directly against the chair.

Tilt the chair backward so that the top of the chair is wedged underneath the doorknob.

The chair buttressed by other furniture will make it extremely difficult to open the door from outside.

BLOCKADE A DOOR THAT OPENS OUTWARD

Using a rope, fishing line, phone cord, or electrical cord, tie the doorknob to the leg of a heavy dresser or other immovable object. Loop the rope around the knob several times so that it will not slip off, and be sure the line to the fixture remains taut. Anyone trying to enter the room will be unable to pull the door open.

Entry Alarm

1 Collect stackable items that will make a noise if toppled.
Empty cans—between 6 and 10—work best. Jars or bottles will also work in an emergency, but the glass might break.

2 Select a door.
Alarm a door other than the one to the room you are in, so that you will have advance warning if someone is coming. For example, alarm the front door if you are in the bedroom.

3 Shut the door.

4 Stack the items against the door.

5 Retreat to your room.
If someone opens the alarmed door, the items will topple and you will have time to prepare for their approach.

Alternate Method

- Tie several cans, cowbells, or Christmas ornaments to the doorknob. When your intruder opens the door, the objects will knock against each other, warning you of an interruption.

HOW TO DEAL WITH A PROMISCUOUS ROOMMATE

⭐ Prearrange a "keep out" signal.
Agree that a towel wrapped around the door handle, a hotel-style "Do Not Disturb" sign, or an index card in the doorjamb indicates the room is occupied and being used, and you should stay out for an agreed-upon period of time. Forty-five minutes should be the maximum.

⭐ Dismantle bunk beds and move your bed far away from his.
You will be less likely to be awakened if your bed frame is not attached to his.

⭐ Pretend that nothing is happening.
Start a conversation with your roommate as though nothing is going on. Ask questions about how his day has been, what he's planning on doing tomorrow, or what he had for dinner. Talk to his hook-up. "I don't believe that we've ever met before. What is your name? What's your major?"

⭐ Play your stereo.
Blast loud, raucous music from your stereo to break your roommate's concentration. Avoid sultry songs that will only provide encouragement.

✪ Watch television.
Wear headphones plugged into your television to block out noise and distract yourself.

✪ Foil future hook-ups.
Be your roommate's shadow at parties. When it appears that a hook-up may be in the offing, quickly intercede when your roommate is distracted. Mention how great it is that the two have gotten together "in light of his recent condition," then be evasive. Comments such as "I hope you have a better time than the others" and "I expect I'll be seeing more of you since I rarely leave the room" will also discourage the hook-up. If all else fails, tell your roommate that you forgot your keys and ask him to walk you home. If he won't leave with you, ask for his keys. When he returns home, you can choose whether or not to unlock the door.

✪ Obtain a date of your own.

How to Silence Squeaky Bedsprings

✪ Lubricate.
When your roommate's bed is not in use, oil the bedsprings and any joints of the bed frame that are visible.

✪ Tighten the nuts and bolts.
Use a wrench to strengthen the bed's framework.

✪ Wrap the bed's joints.
Wrap cotton strips or thick socks around the bed's joints to muffle a squeaking sound. Use duct tape to secure the wrapping in place.

✪ Remove the mattress from the frame.
Encourage your roommate to sleep with the mattress directly on the floor or set it on a thick piece of plywood resting on cinder blocks.

✪ Wear earplugs.
The bed might still squeak, but you won't notice.

✪ Make your own bed squeak.

Inappropriate Music For Sex

Song	Artist or Writer
"Puff the Magic Dragon"	Peter, Paul, and Mary
"Scooby Doo, Where Are You! (theme song)	David Mook and Ben Raleigh
Super Mario Brothers theme song ("Go Go Mario")	Koji Kondo
"The Imperial March" (Darth Vader's Theme)	John Williams
"Grandma Got Run Over by a Reindeer"	Elmo & Patsy
"The Star Spangled Banner"	Francis Scott Key
"Old MacDonald Had a Farm"	Traditional
"Who Let the Dogs Out"	Baha Men
"It's a Small World After All"	Robert and Richard Sherman
"Achy Breaky Heart"	Billy Ray Cyrus
"All by Myself"	Eric Carmen
"The Final Countdown"	Europe
"You're Beautiful"	James Blunt
"Bad Day"	Daniel Powter
"Tie a Yellow Ribbon Round the Ole Oak Tree"	Tony Orlando
"Puttin' on the Ritz"	Taco
"Love Will Keep Us Together"	The Captain and Tenille
"Together Forever"	Rick Astley
"You're Having My Baby"	Paul Anka

HOW TO SURVIVE IF YOU WAKE UP NEXT TO SOMEONE WHOSE NAME YOU DON'T REMEMBER

At Their Place

1 Do not panic.
Evidence of your partner's name exists somewhere nearby. Your task will be to find it before she awakens, or before she starts any sort of meaningful conversation.

2 Get up and go to the bathroom.
The bathroom is a normal place to visit first thing in the morning, and it is also a place where you might discover her name.

3 Look through the medicine cabinet for prescription medicines with her name on the label.

4 Sort through magazines, looking for subscription labels with her name and address.

5 Go through a wastebasket to find discarded junk mail addressed to her.

Look through medicine cabinets for prescription medicines with your date's name on the label.

6 Return to the bedroom.

If she is awake, ask her to make coffee for you. Use the time alone to search the bedroom for evidence. Look for: wallet, checkbook, ID or name bracelet, photo album, scrapbook, business cards (a stack of cards, not just one), or luggage labels. If she is sleeping, look for these and other items throughout the house.

Be Aware
- Try to find at least two items with the same name to be certain that you have identified her, unless the name on one item rings a bell.

AT YOUR PLACE

1 Use terms of endearment when addressing her.
Do not guess at her name. Acceptable terms of endearment are:
- Honey/Sweetie/Cutie
- Darling/Baby/Sugar
- Beautiful/Handsome/Gorgeous

2 Unless you are certain you have ample time, do not go through her belongings.
If your partner is showering, you can count on having at least a few minutes of privacy to search through her belongings. Otherwise, do not risk it—it would be far more embarrassing to be caught searching through her possessions than to admit you cannot remember her name. (She may be in the same predicament.)

3 Ask leading questions while making small talk.
Fishing for information is risky and can backfire by calling attention to what you are trying to do. However, if you feel you can pull it off, try to trick her into revealing her name:
- While getting dressed, pull out your own ID and ask her if she thinks that your hair is better now or in the picture. Laugh about how silly you used to

look. Ask her if she likes the picture on her license. (She may think that you are checking her age.)

- Ask her if she ever had a nickname. She might say, "No, just [Name]."
- Ask her how she got her name.

4 As she is leaving, give her your business card and ask for hers.

If she does not have a business card, ask her to write her vital information on yours. Tell her you may want to send her a little surprise. Do not forget to send something later in the week and make sure that you spell her name correctly.

HOW TO SURVIVE THE WALK OF SHAME

⭐ Locate all your belongings before vacating the premises.

⭐ Replace missing clothing.
If you are lacking pants, put your legs through the sleeves of your shirt and tape or staple the neck. If you are missing a shirt, use your socks as a bikini top, held in place with shoelaces from your running shoes: One lace goes through the top of each sock and is knotted at each end; that lace will go around your neck. The other lace goes through the heel of each sock, is knotted at each end, and becomes the strap that goes behind your back. Adjust for proper fit.

⭐ Dumb down your evening garments.
Remove any showy clothing or jewelry and wash your face to remove any trace of heavy makeup. Wear a hat, sunglasses, and drab clothing, if you have the option.

⭐ Avoid crowds.
Leave for home very early in the morning, when there will be fewer people on the street. If you wake up late, do not cross campus during peak class times.

✪ Walk briskly.
Match the gait of other passersby—but do not run.
The faster you walk, the less likely you'll be noticed.
Walking fast also cuts down on the amount of time
and thus the number of people to whom you will be
exposed.

Be Aware
• Arrange in advance a signal (bird call) to get your
  roommate's attention when you arrive after hours
  with no keys.
• Prepare and practice excuses and explanations for
  parents, boyfriend, and others you may encounter.

How to Avoid a Nightmare Hook-Up

✪ Do not get drunk.
When you need to refill your glass, do it yourself. Do
not let a stranger get a drink for you. Drink a glass of
water between alcoholic drinks.

✪ Clearly convey your desire for a straightforward
hook-up.
Verbalize your desire to hook up with him for that
night. State that you are not interested in pursuing a
relationship of any sort. If he agrees to this, he may be
interested in only a one-night stand as well, and may
be just what you're looking for.

✪ Clear the potential hook-up with a trusted friend.
Always go to a party or bar with a reasonably con-scientious friend who does not have a penchant for drink or proven bad taste in men. Leave your keys with her. Introduce her to your potential hook-up and ask if she thinks you are about to make a mistake.

✪ Retrieve your keys from your friend.

✪ Go to your place.
Your place is usually the preferred destination, since you will be more in charge and comfortable.

✪ Give yourself a last-minute excuse to get out.
Say that your roommates may be home and they would create a problem, so you will have to say good-night right now.

✪ Assess his place.
If you do wind up at his apartment or dorm room, look for signs of misrepresentation or personality disorder. Flip through recent photos to get an idea of his social activities. Lock yourself in the bathroom and check out the contents of his medicine cabinet. Check the bedroom for concealed cameras. If his roommates are home, note whether your hook-up is winking at them or if he politely introduces you by name. Chat with them to make sure you are comfortable in the situation.

✪ **End the encounter.**

If you become uncomfortable or suspicious, leave quickly if you are at his place. If you are at home, say that you forgot that your boyfriend is coming over or that you've got a major headache/infection/test in the morning and need to get a few hours of sleep. If he seems reluctant to leave, give your roommate a sign to rescue you. Do not make any promises, however vague, to see him again.

Be Aware

- Going to your place for a hook-up can be problematic because he will know where you live and he may observe more about you than you would like. Also, you can't get up and leave when you want to end the hook-up.

- If you anticipate that you may be bringing a hook-up home, leave a note taped to your door. "Honey, I went to bed early. Please be quiet when you come in.—Mike." You can then explain later to your hook-up, if you want an excuse to end the evening, that your boyfriend has unexpectedly come over. If you want to continue with the hook-up, you can say that Mike is dating your roommate.

HOW TO DATE THREE PEOPLE AT ONCE

⭐ Assign them the same nickname.
Call them all "honey" or "sweetie" or "pumpkin" so that you do not accidentally use the wrong name with the wrong person. It also helps if you discuss the same topics and pick the same song as "our song."

⭐ Keep to a schedule.
See them only on their assigned day—Mary every Thursday, Emily every Friday, and Jenny every Saturday. They will see you as highly disciplined and will not expect to monopolize your time.

⭐ Select three different favorite bars, activities, or restaurants.
A special place for each reduces your chances of running into another date. Look for dimly lit, off-campus locations.

⭐ Be vague.
Provide few details to each date about your whereabouts during nondate evenings. Offer ambiguous responses like "I wish I had time to see you more often, too."

⭐ Keep your answering machine volume turned down.
If you are home with one of your dates and another calls, you will not be found out.

✪ Advise your roommate to say as little as possible.
Explain your situation and ask for cooperation. Tell your roommate to say only "Nice to see you" when he sees one of your dates. He should avoid "Nice to meet you" or "Nice to see you again" since he may be easily confused about who he is talking to.

✪ Do not place photographs around your room.
The fewer things and people to explain, the better. Also remove stuffed animals, flowers, cards, mix CDs, or anything that might look like a romantic gift.

✪ Tell everyone that you have a large family.
Prepare for the time that you will be spotted with another date. If asked later who you were with, you can say she was your cousin.

✪ Refer to several part-time jobs.
Say that you are sorry to be so unavailable because you are always working. Mention that you are saving all the money you are earning for tuition and other living expenditures so that you don't build expectations about gifts or expensive dates.

✪ Do not boast.
Aside from your roommate, keep any mention of the simultaneous relationships to yourself. The more people you tell about your multiple assignations, the more likely it is that you will be discovered.

HOW TO HOOK UP
IN THE LIBRARY

✪ Scout out a suitable makeout location.

Look for dim lighting and empty aisles in the stacks on a higher floor. Avoid areas near doors, entrances, main aisles, and passenger elevators. Library carrels, stairwells, and freight elevators in out-of-the-way locations are also good options. The oversized book collection features large tables and big, bulky volumes that allow for privacy. Determine less-traveled areas by reviewing the Dewey Decimal System. Sections that begin with the call numbers below are most likely to be quiet:

> 090 Manuscripts and book rarities
> 110 Metaphysics
> 170 Ethics (moral philosophy)
> 210 Natural religion
> 480 Hellenic; Classic Greek
> 510 Mathematics
> 670 Manufactures
> 707 Antiques and collectibles
> 930 General history of the ancient world

Sections with the following call numbers offer more risky locations but may provide some inspiration and atmosphere for the hook-up:

> 440 Romance languages, French
> 577 Pure science: General nature of life
> 618 Gynecology and other medical specialties

757 Painting: Human figures and their parts
770 Photography and photographs
811 Poetry

✪ Time your rendezvous.
Select a time when your designated location will be deserted.

✪ Meet at a predetermined location.
Pass a note to your hook-up target with a time and location. Indicate a specific Dewey Decimal section for the rendezvous.

Be Aware
- Be respectful of the books. Do not damage or misuse them.

HOW TO DISGUISE A FART DURING SEX

⊛ Make a loud exclamation.

At the moment you pass gas, emit a vigorous moan, scream, or exclamation of pleasure (e.g.: Wow! Whoa! Bam!). Continue moaning or screaming until the fart has concluded. Do not scream or moan so loudly that it sounds like you are reaching orgasm.

⊛ Cover the noise with loud physical action.

Pound on the headboard or violently squeak the bed-springs. Swing your arms wildly and knock a lamp or vase off the bedside table.

⊛ Cover the noise with a less objectionable bodily function.

Cough, clear your throat, or sneeze at the moment of farting.

⊛ Take aim.

Disperse the smell by aiming the fart outside of the bed linens. If you and your partner are having sex under the covers, angle your butt up and out of them just before the fart emerges, so the smell does not become trapped and linger.

⊛ Mask the smell with sexually suggestive smells.

Immediately after passing gas—but before the smell becomes pervasive—jump up and light scented candles,

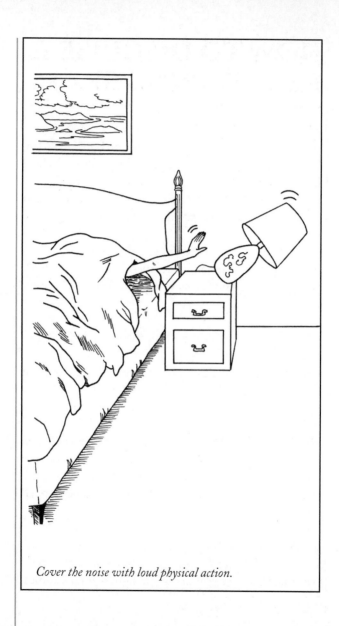

Cover the noise with loud physical action.

chapter 4: getting it on

or introduce a strongly smelling foodstuff (such as melted chocolate, scented liqueur, or Camembert cheese) into your lovemaking.

★ Pretend it was the dog.
If your dog is not in the room, say he must have run out after farting.

★ Distract from the fart with something more outlandish.
As you feel the need to fart approaching, start making a loud farting noise with your mouth; continue making the noise until after your actual fart. If questioned about the noise, whether in the moment or after sex, explain that you have a thing for motorboats.

★ Laugh and keep going.

HOW TO SURVIVE CALLING OUT THE WRONG NAME

⭐ Be honest.
Immediately apologize for hurting your partner's feelings. Do not say "What? I didn't say anything," or try to pretend that your partner misheard. Lying will just make the situation worse.

⭐ Plead insanity.
Portray the accident as the result of the extreme pleasure the sex was providing you. Say, "I was so turned on I totally lost my mind for a second."

⭐ Blame it on habit.
Your partner may not be thrilled, but your partner should understand you've been with other people before. Explain that the name you called instead of hers belongs to a former partner, and you must have yelled it out from old habit.

⭐ Give your partner a compliment.
Say, "It's just so weird that I called you that. You're so much hotter than her/better than her in bed!" Look your partner in the eye as you are saying it. Crinkle your eyes and shake your head. Appear genuinely baffled.

✪ Laugh about it.
The more seriously you appear to take the infraction, the more serious a problem your partner will consider it to be. Smile, laugh a little, and say, "It is kind of funny, isn't it?" If your partner is not laughing, stop laughing.

✪ Do not re-initiate activity.
You may be anxious to begin again, both to move past the wrong-name-calling and to reach the climax you were approaching when the error occurred. But unless your partner laughs off the incident and makes the first move, do not attempt to re-engage.

✪ Give your partner some time.
Calling out someone else's name while in bed with a long-time partner will bruise his or her ego, and may cause upset for a while. But if you haven't given any other cause to fear your infidelity, eventually this minor *faux pas* will be forgotten. It may be that your partner had also been thinking of someone else at the time, and may not be as upset as you imagine.

HOW TO HIDE UNATTRACTIVE FEATURES

✪ Dim the lights.
Turn off as many lights as possible in the bedroom, car, or backstage area.

✪ Change the lights.
Say you'd like to establish a "mood," by employing a strobe light, disco ball, darkroom lighting, black-lights, light from a flashing motel sign through venetian blinds, or any other form of room lighting that makes it extremely difficult to see.

✪ Blindfold your partner.
Establish a "safe word" which will cue you to untie the blindfold.

✪ Mask your partner.
Give your partner a mask with very small eyeholes. Tell your partner you have a thing for the Star Wars character Jar Jar Binks, Richard Nixon, or clowns; or for Bono, and you can only make love to someone who is wearing wraparound sunglasses.

✪ Wear a costume.
Many sexually-intended or fetish costumes will cover up most or all of your body, while still allowing for sexual activity to take place.

Give your partner a mask with very small eyeholes.

✪ **Keep clothes on over your unattractive parts.**
Explain that you can only become sexually aroused when partially or fully dressed.

✪ **Initiate a sexual position where the offending parts are hidden.**
If you are uncomfortable with your chest, insist on having sex facing away from your partner. If it is your feet you do not like, have your partner on top of you so he cannot see them.

✪ **Have sex over the phone, or online.**
Select an avatar whose body is better than yours.

HOW TO TREAT PASSION INJURIES

SCRATCHES

1 Apply pressure.
Hold a clean cloth or fresh bed sheet against the scratch.

2 Clean the injury.
Flush out the scratch mark with warm water and a little bit of mild soap.

3 Allow the wound to air-dry.
Continue having sex while the wound dries; the vigorous motion will cause it to dry faster. If you begin perspiring into the wound, stop.

4 Put on a bandage.
When the wound is dry, cover the scratch completely with a bandage.

BITE MARKS

1 Run water over the wound.
Run cold, clean water over the bite.

2 Clean the wound with soap and water.
Use a mild household soap. Do not use alcohol, per-

oxide, or anything else that causes the bite to burn or sting.

3 | Apply ice.
Wrap ice or a chilled bottle of champagne in a damp towel and press it against the wounded area.

4 | Elevate the affected area above the level of the heart.
If you have been bitten in the genitals, buttocks, or other below-the-belt area, lie flat with your lower body on a 15-degree incline.

5 | Put pressure on the affected area for 10 minutes.
Leave the ice-pack pressed against the skin for at least 10 minutes.

6 | Resume activity.

Be Aware
• Human bites have a higher rate of infection than bites from animals, especially if they break the skin. Bites on the hands carry the highest risk of complications. Anyone with a severe bite should see a doctor. Signs of infection from a human bite include redness, pus, tenderness, and inflammation.

Sprains And Strains

Overstretched or torn ligaments (sprains) muscles and tendons (strains) can result from sudden motion or overextension.

1 Lie down.
Remove any weight or pressure on the injured area and allow it to rest.

2 Apply a cold compress.
Cold will constrict blood vessels and reduce swelling. Place ice in a plastic bag or wrap it in a towel or bedsheet. Do not apply the compress directly to the skin. Apply for 30 minutes. If the sprain or strain is particularly bad and swelling is rapid and severe, leave the compress on for an additional 15 minutes.

3 Make a pressure bandage.
If no emergency bandage is available, or will fit the area of the injury, tear strips from the bedsheets long enough to wrap and bind the area to physically compress the area and reduce swelling while not cutting off blood flow.

4 Elevate the injured area.
Raise the injured area above the heart as often as possible over the next two days.

5 Take ibuprofen to reduce swelling and relieve pain.
If ibuprofen is not available, take acetaminophen, which will relieve pain but not swelling. Avoid aspirin, which can thin the blood.

6 Proceed with caution.
Limit or avoid activity involving the injury site and gently exercise the area over the next days to weeks until use of the area feels normal.

Be Aware

- Seek medical attention if the injury site remains severely painful, is immobilized, numb, exhibits redness extending from the injury area, or appears misshapen in comparison to an analogous uninjured limb or joint.

HOW TO SURVIVE A "MISFIRE"

1 Apologize.
Say you are sorry and that you feel badly. Do not lie; specifically, do not say "this has never happened to me before," even if it has never happened to you before.

2 Make it a compliment.
Tell your partner, "I'm sorry honey—I'm just so attracted to you that I become overstimulated. Let's figure out together how to get more in synch."

3 Attend to your partner's needs.
Continue to pleasure your partner with other sexual (non-intercourse) favors until your partner is satisfied.

4 Try again.
Most men will perform longer the second or third time around.

5 Address your issues.
Seek out psychological help, if necessary.

Be Aware
- On average men ejaculate after five minutes of penetration.
- 25 to 40 percent of men report premature ejaculation.

- The roots of premature ejaculation can be psychological, and can be treated through psychotherapy and relationship therapy. Unhealthy relationships, sexual hang-ups or fears, and many other anxieties and stresses can cause premature ejaculation, and should be addressed accordingly.

How to Avoid a Misfire

1 Pre-party.
In the hour before an anticipated sexual encounter, masturbate to extend the period before your body will be ready to orgasm again. If you drink alcohol, have a drink; alcohol in moderation can dull your sexual response and slow things down.

2 Distract yourself.
Perform complicated mental exercises, such as listing the letters of the alphabet in reverse order, or doing complex addition (e.g. adding 1 to 2 to 3 to 4 . . .)

3 Think boring or unsexy thoughts.
Think about household chores you don't enjoy. Relive your most embarrassing moments, ranked and sorted by different phases of your life (childhood, adolescence, college . . .) Think about dreary, work-related problems, unless they involve sexy coworkers.

4 Mentally repeat a mantra.
Silently chant a meaningless made-up phrase or a particularly memorable but unsexy commercial jingle in

your mind during the sexual act. Focus all your mental energy on the syllables of the phrase.

5 Breathe deeply.
Oxygenating your blood can help focus your attention and calm your mind.

6 Make noise.
Moaning and screaming during sex can release pent up tension and delay orgasm. It may also please your partner and bring you closer in sync.

7 Get uncomfortable.
Change position to anything less comfortable than what you're doing. If this becomes comfortable, change again.

8 Stop.
When you feel your orgasm coming, stop what you are doing and wait for the feeling to pass. Reengage when you feel ready.

ANTIAPHRODESIACS

FOOD	WHY IT KILLS YOUR SEX DRIVE:
Black Licorice	Certain types of black licorice contain glycyrrhizin which reduces testosterone levels (testosterone is necessary for the sex drive in both men and women)
Gin and Tonic	Alcoholic beverages and quinine (a key ingredient in tonic) both diminish the sex drive
Salt	Causes high blood pressure which can result in erectile dysfunction
Soy	Promotes estrogen increases and a subsequent testosterone reduction;
Sugar	Testosterone levels can be reduced by as much as 25% when blood sugar spikes
Too much food	Overindulging causes blood sugar levels to go out of balance and devote blood to the stomach

STRANGE ANIMAL MATING HABITS

ANIMAL	BEHAVIOR
Bonobo Apes	Use sex or sexual behavior to resolve all disputes rather than fighting; they are lovers, not fighters
Flatworms	Flatworms are hermaphrodites (they have both male and female organs) and "fence" each other with their penises; the loser is impregnated
Porcupines	The male urinates on the female; if she wants to mate she will expose her quill-free underside; if not, she will shake off the urine
Macaques	Will pay (with fruit) to get a look at the female macaques' hind quarters
Sea Hares	Also hermaphrodites, these sea slugs mate in a chain, forming a sex circle

chapter 4: getting it on

HOW TO SURVIVE GETTING STUCK IN A POSITION

A muscle lock-up or "charlie horse" can occur when overdoing physical activity or engaging in activity when muscles are cold, or when the body suffers from dehydration or a lack of electrolytes.

1 Stop what you're doing.
Stop whatever activity immediately preceded the muscle lock.

2 Disengage.
Have the still-mobile partner extract themselves from the position, disturbing the position of the locked partner as little as possible.

3 Press or stretch the affected area.
Push gently on the affected limb, jaw, or muscle group to help release the immediate pain of the lock hold for one minute. The affected partner should try to keep breathing regular and deep to continue oxygenating the blood.

4 Massage the area.
Massage the affected area in a slow kneading motion to facilitate blood flow and warm the muscles.

how to survive getting stuck in a position

5 Apply heat.
If pain has not eased, apply a warm compress or heating pad to the area.

6 Drink water.
Have the affected partner drink a glass of water to offset effects of dehydration.

7 Rest.
The strained muscle is likely to remain tender for some time. Wait several hours and begin gently before resuming amorous activity.

Be Aware

- To minimize the risk of muscle cramping, drink plenty of water, and maintain a balanced diet including foods rich in sodium and electrolytes (including, bananas, potatoes, and whole grains) before engaging in sexual activity.

HOW TO SHUSH A SCREAMER

1   Eroticize the forbidden.

If sex becomes necessary in a place where noise could prove problematic, make the need for total quiet a part of the sexual play. Pretend you are in hiding, or strangers on a train.

2   Establish control breathing.

As sexual arousal begins to build, breathe deeply in and out, focusing all of your energy on not screaming. Show your partner that you are doing these "focusing breaths," and encourage her to model your behavior. Breathe together in sync, looking in one another's eyes.

3   Silently scream.

Whisper to your partner to pretend to scream, without actually emitting any noise. Pretend-scream back at her; make it a game, seeing who can make the most vigorous silent scream.

4   Offer something to bite down on.

When you see that a real scream is building, have your partner stuff a pillow, blanket, hand, or other item in her mouth to clamp her teeth down on instead.

5 Mask the noise.

If screaming still occurs, cover it with louder noises, such as hair dryers, bath tubs being filled up, and blasting radios and televisions.

Appropriate vs. Inappropriate Things to Shout Out During Sex	
Appropriate	**Inappropriate**
I love you!	I loved you!
I'm going to come!	I'm going to pretend to come!
I want to make you come!	I want to break up with you!
You look amazing!	You look kind of familiar!
You look so hot!	You look sort of like my mom!
More! More!	Are you almost done?
Yes! Yes!	Shut up! Shut up! Won't you please shut up!
Does that feel good?	What's the name of that restaurant with the really good garlic bread?

HOW TO BRING UP YOUR FETISH OR KINK

1 | Do your research.
Know as much as possible about the fetish, including safety issues, equipment requirements, and cost, before you bring it up to your partner, so you can articulately answer any questions he may have.

2 | Choose a good time.
Wait until your partner is in a good, relaxed mood, perhaps after sex. Do not bring it up right before sex. Definitely do not bring it up in the middle of sex.

3 | Test the waters.
Say "Oh, I had the craziest thought," or "I had the wildest dream about you," and explain that in the dream he was participating with you in this surprising or unusual sexual act.

4 | Try a joke.
Put the kink or fetish in the context of, "Wouldn't it be hilarious if . . ." or "You know what would be so funny? . . ."

5 | Introduce by example.
Watch for opportunities to segue into the conversation, such as the kink being mentioned in a TV program or

film, or actively seek out such a show or movie and see how he reacts.

6 | Be honest.
Now that the subject has been opened, tell him honestly and specifically what it is you want to do, and what his role will be.

7 | Make it a two-way street.
Encourage your partner to tell you if there is anything unusual or out of the mainstream that he wants to try. Do not freak out.

8 | Have a sense of humor.
On the first few attempts at acting out your fetish or kink, allow yourself and your partner to have some embarrassment or awkwardness about the new activity.

UNUSUAL SEXUAL FETISHES

Name	Description
Agalmatophilia	Sexual obsession with statues or mannequins
Chelonaphilia	Sexual obsession with turtles
Coulrophilia	Sexual obsession with clowns
Dendrophilia	Sexual obsession with trees
Dracophilia	Sexual obsession with dragons
Eproctophilia	Sexual obsession with flatulence
Extrophilia	Sexual obsession with aliens
Faunoiphilia	Sexual obsession with watching animals mate
Formicophilia	Sexual obsession with insects crawling on genitalia
Hobophilia	Sexual obsession with hobos
Kakorrhaphiphilia	Sexual obsession with failure
Mechanophilia	Sexual obsession with cars and other machines
Plushophilia	Sexual obsession with stuffed animals or people in plush costumes
Schediaphilia (aka Toonophilia)	Sexual obsession with cartoons
Siderodromophilia	Sexual obsession with trains
Spectrophili	Sexual obsession with ghosts
Taphephilia	Sexual obsession with being buried alive
Tripsolagnia	Sexual obsession with having your hair shampooed by someone else
Ursusagalmatophilia	Sexual obsession with teddy bears

HOW TO SURVIVE GETTING THE GIGGLES

1 Give in.
The effort of trying to suppress laughs may translate into diminished performance. Instead of suppressing the urge to giggle, let them out.

2 Reassure your partner with science.
If your partner is confused or put off by your laughter, assure him that the giggling has nothing to do with his looks or performance, but is a purely inadvertent, physical response to anxiety, arousal, or adrenaline. (Say this even if your laughter is a result of his looks or performance).

3 Blame it on ticklishness.
Tell your partner he touched a part of your body that is extremely ticklish.

4 Offer a compliment.
Use the giggling as the basis for a kind remark, such as "I'm laughing at my good luck to be with someone as attractive as you are."

5 Invite participation.

Ask your partner to start giggling also, and continue giggling as you continue sexual activity. Where you would normally shout or moan with pleasure, laugh instead.

How To Avoid The Giggles

1 Slow down.

As you feel the fit of giggling approach, pause in your activities and focus your attention on not laughing.

2 Look away.

The intimacy anxiety that sometimes provokes giggles can be minimized by eliminating eye contact with your partner. Close your eyes, or look at the headboard or out the window.

3 Avoid conversation.

Do not attempt dirty talk or express verbal enthusiasm.

4 Breathe deeply.

Close your eyes and inhale through your nose.

5 Hold your breath for a count of five.

6 Exhale fully through your mouth.

Repeat steps 3 to 5 until the urge to giggle subsides.

Be Aware

- Giggling during sex can result from adrenaline and arousal; from nervousness about intimacy and performance; or from simple ticklishness. Certain areas of the body, especially along the legs and upper thighs, become even more sensitized during sex.
- If you have a history of getting giggly during sexual encounters, warn new partners in advance to minimize the potential for bruised egos.
- The Inuit Eskimo expression for sex translates as "laughing time."

HOW TO HAVE SEX IN A SMALL SPACE

AIRPLANE LAVATORY

1 Pick a rendezvous time.

Select a time when you are least likely to have to wait in line and when you will not be disturbed. The best times are just before the plane reaches cruising altitude or during the in-flight entertainment.

2 As the plane is ascending, listen for a beep from the in-flight messaging system.

The first beep comes without a subsequent announcement and indicates to the flight attendants that cruising altitude has almost been reached and that it is safe to begin their preparations. The fasten your seatbelt sign will still be illuminated, but the flight attendants will get up. As soon as the flight attendants clear the aisle, head for the lavatory. Try to select one that is not visible from the galleys. Have your date wait at least a minute, then meet you in the lavatory. You should hear the beverage carts roll by. After a few minutes, the flight attendants will begin to serve drinks, blocking the aisle from passenger access. Alternatively, or in addition, proceed to step 3.

3 Meet during the movie.

Plan your rendezvous for the beginning of the film, preferably when the film is at least fifteen minutes underway. Most passengers and flight attendants stay out of the aisles and galley areas during the entertainment portion of the flight, so you will have more privacy. You should proceed to the lavatory first, to be followed a minute later by your date.

4 | Put down the toilet seat lid and clean it.
Wipe the seat with sani-wipes if they are available, or use a wet paper towel with soap. Place paper towels or a sanitary toilet seat cover on top for extra protection.

5 | Be quiet and be quick.
You will not have a lot of time before people are lining up to get into the restroom.

6 | Be ready for turbulence.
The safest positions involve one partner sitting on the closed toilet seat. Then, in the event of bumpy air, neither partner will be too close to the ceiling, risking a concussion.

7 | If you do encounter turbulence, hold on.
Brace yourself against the sink and do not try to stand up or move. Stay where you are and ride it out.

8 | Exit the lavatory together, feigning illness.
It is illegal to have sex in an airplane bathroom—so deny it in the unlikely event that you are asked. Tell the flight attendant or other passengers that one of you was ill and the other was offering assistance.

Elevator

1 Find a building with an older elevator.

Many older elevators have an emergency stop button that will allow you to halt the elevator. On other units, flipping the switch from run to stop will cause an alarm bell to sound. You will still have plenty of time, at least ten or fifteen minutes, possibly as long as an hour, before firefighters or other emergency personnel are able to access the elevator cabin.

2 Alternatively, look for a freight elevator with padding on the walls.

Freight elevators will be less likely to have an alarm that sounds when the stop switch is thrown. The padding may also muffle sound and provide comfort.

3 Look for a camera.

Virtually all new elevators have security cameras, as do some older ones, including freight elevators. If a camera is present, cover the camera lens—it will probably be in a rear corner—with a piece of tape or with several postage stamps. The security system may include audio as well, however.

4 Stop the elevator between floors.

Elevator doors house a mechanical clutch that opens the corridor (outer) doors. If the elevator is not level with a floor, the corridor doors cannot open, and someone from the outside will not easily be able to open the inner doors.

5 | Release the stop button or flip the switch to run when you are ready to leave.

Exit the elevator normally. If emergency personnel are present, tell them there was a malfunction but that you are okay.

Be Aware
• If the elevator is stopped level with a floor, an elevator technician will be able to open both the outer (corridor) doors and the inner (elevator) doors from the outside.

DRESSING ROOM

1 | Look for a dressing room that has a door and walls that extend to the floor.

If all the dressing rooms have a gap between the floor and the walls, look for one with a secure door, rather than a curtain. If you are in a store that has several dressing rooms, look for the least-trafficked or least-monitored areas. Some dressing rooms have very hard-to-detect security systems—including two-way mirrors—so you cannot guarantee that you will not be seen.

2 | Carry clothes as if you are going to try them on.

Trail after a demanding customer who is requiring the attentions of the sales associate on duty. When the employee is occupied, make your move and duck into the dressing room.

3 | Have your partner follow behind a few minutes later.

4 | Be quiet.
The walls to dressing rooms are thin.

5 | Be quick.
Speed is important, especially if your legs are visible beneath the walls.

6 | Depart from the dressing room one person at a time. Check your appearance in the mirror, and leave the store's clothes in the dressing room. If you are in the women's section of a department store, the woman should leave first and make sure the coast is clear. If you are in the men's department, the man should leave first.

Be Aware

- For speed and efficiency in airplanes, elevators, and dressing rooms, be sure to wear loose, baggy clothing. Do not wear underwear.

HOW TO HAVE SEX OUTDOORS

While Hiking

1   Find a shelter.
Look for a cluster of bushes, a cavern, or a boulder large enough to shield you from fellow hikers.

2   Clear the ground.
Sweep the area for sticks, sharp rocks, broken glass, or other uncomfortable objects. Avoid areas with ant hills—raised mounds of dirt with a central hole. Place a blanket on the cleared area.

3   Apply sunscreen.
If you will be exposing areas of your body not usually exposed to the sun, apply sunscreen to them, even if you think that the exposure will not be or lengthy duration. Infrequently exposed areas can burn quickly.

4   Watch out for poison ivy.
Poison ivy is a green plant that grows to about two feet high with a cluster of three almond-shaped leaves, often dotted with small white berries. Skin contact with it and poison oak, which also features leaves in groups of three, can result in an uncomfortable allergic reaction and rash. Follow the old scouting motto, "if leaves of three, let it be." Wash with water within five

Poison ivy

Poison oak

Poison sumac

Avoid bare skin contact with these plants, which will result in itching and irritation.

minutes of contact, and treat with ice packs and cala-
mine lotion later to soothe symptoms.

5 Remain quiet.
Many people go to the wilderness in search of peace
and quiet, so your passionate shouts may attract
unwelcome attention from people or animals.

6 Be alert for predators.
Bears can be attracted to unusual scents, including the
scent of human sexual intercourse. If you do see a bear,
stay perfectly still and hope the bear leaves. If attacked,
strike back with anything you can, aiming for the eyes
or snout.

At the Beach

1 Find a semi-enclosed space.
Select a private or deserted beach during the day or
wait until nightfall. Open a large beach umbrella or
hide behind a dune. If out in the open, be aware of
potential views from above, such as from nearby mul-
tistory hotels or nearby parasailers.

2 Prepare the ground.
Sweep the ground for shells or other sharp debris
and lay down a blanket large enough to accommo-
date yourselves with a margin of several feet around
between you and the sand. Watch the area for sand
crabs or mites before setting up.

Beware of outdoor hazards:

voyeurs

crabs

sand mites
(shown not to scale)

sharp shells

3 | Watch the shoreline.
Select a spot many yards inland above the furthest wet tide line to minimize the chances of being swamped, and position at least one of you to be able to see the water if you are active at time of incoming high tide.

4 | Be discrete.
Sound may carry farther than you think depending on the acoustics of the beach terrain. If you need to make sounds but are nervous of being overheard, disguise the sounds as seagull cries or sea lion calls.

5 | Watch for animals in the water.
If you are having sex in the ocean, keep an eye out for sharks, jellyfish, or sting rays. Some animals, such as sharks, are particularly attracted to the splashes, and may investigate unfamiliar scents.

6 | Rinse off.
Sand and other foreign substances pose a risk of infection. When you are finished, rinse off thoroughly, all over, with clean fresh water.

HOW TO SURVIVE FALLING OUT OF A SWING

IF YOU HAVE FALLEN OUT

1 Check for injury.
Feel yourself from top to bottom for potential serious injury. Run your hands along your body looking for open wounds, blood, or bruising. If you are bleeding heavily or have significant pain and tenderness, get dressed and go to the emergency room.

IF YOU ARE FALLING OUT

1 Prepare the ground for dismount.
If you are hanging upside down from a door-way mounted swing, have your partner drag a mattress, pillows or a sleeping bag into the doorway and place them directly beneath you.

2 Untangle or cut yourself free.
Unwind the straps of the harness if they have ensnared you. If necessary, use scissors or a knife to cut away straps that are restraining you.

3 Have your partner gently lower you to the floor.

4 | Check the swing for damage.
If you were using a swing suspended from a free-standing metal frame, test the metal all the way around the swing to make sure it hasn't been cracked or bent by your accident. A bend in the frame means the swing is much more likely to give way easily in the future.

5 | Re-assemble.
Refer to the assembly instructions before putting the swing back together. If you were forced to cut yourself free, do not use the swing again until you can purchase a new harness and seat. Do not rebuild the swing with duct tape or improvised materials you might have around the house.

6 | Get back to work.
Have your partner resume activity gently at first to make sure the reassembled harness is holding your weight, and that the swing retains its structural integrity.

INSTANT SOLUTION

HOW TO SURVIVE LOSING A HANDCUFF KEY

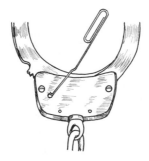

Insert the tip of the pick into the lock.

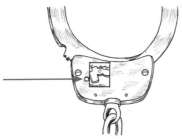

*Turn the pick left and right to move the latch
and unlock the cuffs.*

*Have the non-handcuffed partner make a pick by bending a paperclip to
straighten one end, then bending a few millimeters of that end 90 degrees.
Fit the pick in the lock and turn to unlock. Alternatively, purchase a new
set of handcuffs and use its key, since most commercially available pairs use
the same one.*

HOW TO PERFORM CPR

1   Check for a response.
Tap your partner on the feet and pull his hair. If he comes to, hold him gently until he feels able to move. Do not resume sexual activity.

2   Get in position.
If your partner is not breathing and his heart is not beating, take him off the bed and lay him out on a flat firm surface such as the floor. Kneel down next to him. Take off anything that might restrict breathing, such as a dog collar or mask.

3   Give rescue breaths.
Put your fingers under his chin and push up gently, tilting his head back. Pinch his nose closed and cover his mouth with your own. Give two long breaths into his mouth; watch his chest to be sure it rises and falls with your breaths.

4   Give chest compressions.
Put the heel of your right hand in the center of his chest, directly between the nipples. Place your left hand on top of the right and lock your elbows together. Push down hard, using the weight of your body, 30 times.

5 Repeat rescue breaths.
Give two more deep breaths into your partner's mouth, watching his chest to make sure it rises with your breaths.

6 Repeat chest compressions.
Give another 30 swift compressions.

7 Call for help.
After performing five cycles of breaths and compressions, call for emergency assistance. Put your phone on speaker phone so you can continue to perform CPR while on the phone.

8 Keep going.
Continue performing CPR until help arrives or your partner revives.

Be Aware

- Approximately 95 percent of cardiac arrest victims die before they make it to a hospital.
- Effective CPR, provided immediately after cardiac arrest, doubles the chance of survival.
- You may hear an alarming snapping sound while performing chest compressions. Broken ribs are an unfortunate side-effect of CPR, but are preferable to dying.

CHAPTER 5

RELATIONSHIP
SURVIVAL SKILLS

HOW TO SURVIVE IF YOU RUN INTO YOUR EX

Running into your ex at a party can be problematic for many reasons: lingering affection, pain over being dumped, unresolved emotions, passionate memories, or poor selection of your current date.

1 Do not avert your gaze.
Look him in the eye and smile. Shying away from eye contact only diminishes your power. Keep someone's gaze and you keep control.

2 Be nice.

3 Do not sit.
Do not let yourself get stuck in a corner or on a couch with your ex. Remain standing and be ready to move.

4 Take charge of the conversation.
Start by mentioning something that you noticed earlier in the day. This keeps the dialogue fresh and superficial and in your control, and helps you to avoid complimenting or talking about the ex. Be upbeat—enthusiasm is a handy tool. Breezing by someone indicates you are not fazed or upset.

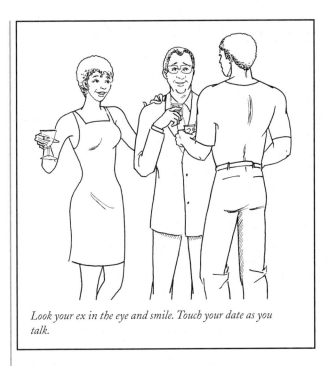

Look your ex in the eye and smile. Touch your date as you talk.

5 Introduce your date and send clear signals that this is who you are with now.

Touch your date as you converse with your ex, making it clear that you have moved on.

6 Keep your conversation short and sweet.

Tell your ex that you are "meeting friends," but that it was nice to see him. Or, tug your date's arm and say, "Oh look, there's Sally. I want you to meet her."

7 Move on.

HOW TO SURVIVE MEETING THE PARENTS

1 Pay attention to your surroundings.
If you are prone to spilling things or tripping over rugs, move slowly and carefully. Present an image of confidence and poise.

2 Greet them with a firm, but brief, handshake.
A weak handshake is a turnoff, but so is squeezing too hard. Shake hands so that the entire hand is clasped. Let go of the hand after a few pumps. Maintain eye contact.

3 Do not kiss or hug the parents unless they make the first move.
If they offer air kisses, fine, but never kiss a potential in-law on the mouth. If they opt to hug you, do not retreat from it.

4 Call them "Mr." and "Mrs." unless they ask you to address them by their first names.
This shows respect. Do not shorten or change their names or call them "Mom" or "Dad."

5 Give them personal space.
Allow at least three feet of airspace during conversation.

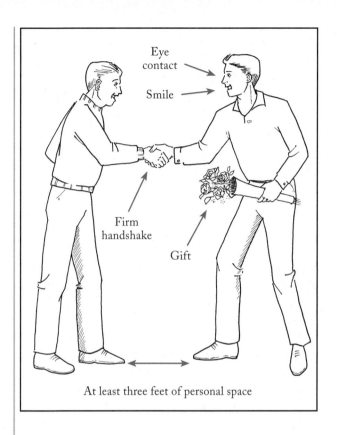

Eye contact

Smile

Firm handshake

Gift

At least three feet of personal space

6 Show poise.

Be positive, good natured, and relaxed. Smile, but not continuously: if you look happy all of the time, something's not right. Remember that good posture projects confidence and successfulness. Walk, stand, and sit up straight. Speak loud enough to be heard.

7 Be sincere and be yourself.

Do not pretend to be someone you are not. People can spot a fake a mile away. Do not try too hard to make an impression. At the same time, do not act too familiar—no winking, shoulder punching, or joking. Follow their lead.

8 Send a note or card the next day.

Mention how nice it was to finally meet them and that you look forward to seeing them again. If you stayed at their house for a while, thank them for an enjoyable visit.

Be Aware

Practicing the following social graces can help make a favorable impression:

- Ring the doorbell once only. Do not lean on the bell or pound the door.
- Turn off your cell phone and pager.
- If invited to dinner, bring wine, flowers, or dessert, even if they say not to.
- Wait to be invited inside, and wait to be seated. Do not sit down before they do.
- Pet the dog or cat.
- Compliment them on only one or two things: the view, the couch, a painting, the flowers—don't overdo it.
- Do not spend too much time in the bathroom (and do not go too often).

HOW TO SURVIVE IF YOU FORGET A BIRTHDAY

1 Apologize. Apologize. Apologize.
Your apology might have to take several forms—flowers, verbal protestations, love letters, a special dinner. Be creative.

2 Accept responsibility for your error.
Recognize sincerely that you blew it. Excuses will only make things worse.

3 Acknowledge your partner's feelings.
Accept your partner's anger as valid and do not question or challenge any reaction. Say, "I can only begin to imagine how you must feel."

4 Plan a special event to fix the mistake.
A weekend getaway, a night at a fancy hotel, or an extremely thoughtful gift will be necessary. However, do not show up two days late with a windfall of gifts, expecting that all will be forgiven. All the presents in the world cannot eliminate the need for talking the matter through.

HOW TO APOLOGIZE WHEN YOU DON'T KNOW WHAT YOU'VE DONE WRONG

1 Evaluate the threat level.

Examine your partner's pupils and nostrils. Pupils dilated/nostrils flared means that you are in an extreme amount of trouble. If the pupils are not dilated, and nostrils are not flared, make a small silly joke or offer a nonsexual compliment and see if a smile is offered. An apology may not be required.

2 Do not guess.

Do not panic and start apologizing for things which your partner may not in fact be aware of. By saying, "I am sorry I was late paying the mortgage," when she may not have known that, may put you in twice as much trouble as before.

3 Offer a nonspecific apology.

"I'm sorry for what I did. What I did was bad. It was a dumb thing to do."

4 Offer a nonspecific excuse.

"I had a lot on my mind when I did that, which was dumb and bad."

5 Solicit information.

Trick your partner into filling you in on what you have done wrong by feigning interest in learning how to do it better next time. "Why don't you tell me exactly what it was that bothered you so much, so I never do it again." Once it is clear what you did, offer an event-specific apology and/or excuse.

6 Offer a guarantee of universally improved performance in future.

Promise that you will do better in all aspects, in all ways, from now on.

Emergency Phrases for When You're in the Doghouse

- "You look so cute/young/thin when you're mad."
- "I was just thinking, we haven't been to [insert name of partner's favorite restaurant] in ages."
- "You know what I suddenly feel like doing? Vacuuming/Cooking/Watching the kids while you get your nails done."
- "In the long run, this isn't going to seem like such a big deal."
- "I got you flowers/a necklace/flowers and a diamond necklace."
- "The important thing is that we have each other."
- "What? What? Where am I? I feel so strange . . . like all the events of the last few days were the result of some sort of alien that took control of my mind."

Phrase of Last Resort: "I was wrong."

how to apologize when you don't know what you've done wrong

HOW TO SURVIVE SNORING

✪ Keep your date on her side or stomach.
Sleeping on the back tends to lead to snoring. If your date falls asleep on her back, change her position using one of the following techniques:
- The Pillow Lift: Grab the nearest corner of the pillow (the corner she is facing, if she is on her side) and lift it up until she begins to rustle and turn over. This may cause her to wake up momentarily and stop snoring.
- The Bed Flop: Actively flip yourself over (from one side to the other, or from your stomach to your back) with an unusually aggressive flop. Make it forceful enough to shake the bed. Often this will disturb her just enough to cause her to turn over as well.

✪ Wake up your date.
If the more subtle approaches do not work, become more aggressive. A strategically placed elbow nudge or kick may awaken your date. Repeat until effective.

✪ Use earplugs.
Be prepared for the worst—have earplugs handy. If you do not have earplugs, try using a small amount of wadded-up cotton from a cotton ball, or even toilet paper. Your final alternative is to sleep in separate

rooms. It may not be romantic, but it is an effective temporary solution.

Be Aware
- Drinking alcohol promotes snoring, so prevent your date from drinking too much. Alcohol depresses the activity of nerves in the nasal air passages, enervating the airway muscles that would keep the air passages open at night and prevent snoring.
- Drinking coffee reduces snoring. Caffeine may stimulate the airway nerves, keeping them open. Caffeine may also make a person sleep more lightly, which can reduce snoring.

HOW TO FIND A PARTNER WHO IS LESS LIKELY TO SNORE

- Avoid the obese, as they have a higher incidence of snoring.
- Avoid individuals with short, fat necks, as these people also have a higher incidence of snoring.
- Avoid individuals who are constantly sniffing and snorting; this may indicate a chronic sinus condition that can cause snoring.
- Avoid heavy drinkers; high alcohol intake leads to a higher incidence of snoring.
- Avoid someone who consistently falls asleep in social situations. Tiredness may be a sign that this person is experiencing reduced quality of sleep due to a sleep disorder that may include snoring.

How to Prevent Snoring

⊗ Change sleep positions.
Snoring is often caused by lying on your back. Train yourself to sleep on your side or stomach.

⊗ Sew a tennis ball to the back of your pajamas.
Prevent yourself from turning over onto your back in the middle of the night by attaching a tennis ball to your back. This will force you to lie on your side, effectively ridding you of the habit.

⊗ Avoid alcohol.
Alcohol and other sedatives increase muscle relaxation, which increases snoring.

⊗ Change your diet.
Reduce the amount of refined carbohydrates and dairy products that you consume. Both increase mucus production which can cause snoring. Also avoid eating large meals at night right before bed.

⊗ Exercise.
Extra body fat, especially bulky neck tissue, can cause snoring. Losing just 10 percent of your body weight can improve your overall breathing.

⊗ Apply nasal strips.
Open nasal passages with adhesive nose strips.

Sew a tennis ball to the back of your pajamas.

how to survive snoring

✪ Use a throat spray.
Lubricate your throat with a spray that will relax the throat muscles.

✪ Practice aromatherapy.
Reduce nasal congestion with essential oils. Leave a jar of majoram oil open on your nightstand while you sleep. Add a few drops of eucalyptus oil to a water-filled humidifier. Breathe in the steam just prior to going to bed.

✪ Use a neti pot.
Reduce allergens in your sinuses by washing out your nasal passages with a neti pot. Fill the pot with water and ¼ teaspoon of salt. Hold your head over a sink at an angle so your chin is parallel with your forehead. Tilt the pot so the tip of the arm enters one nostril. Allow the water to flow in one nostril and out the other. Repeat in the other nostril.

✪ Prop up your mattress.
Put a dictionary, encyclopedia, or phone book under your mattress to raise your head and change the angle of your neck.

HOW TO DEAL WITH A CHEATING LOVER

1 Ask her outright.

If you suspect your lover is cheating on you, do not worry about embarrassment or gathering too much evidence. The fact that you are unsure of her fidelity is enough to raise the issue. If she expresses surprise by the question or hesitates, present your reasons for asking in as calm a way as possible.

2 Do not act impulsively and end the relationship.

If you ascertain that she is cheating on you, all is not lost. Talk or cry together, and then spend some time apart. If this is the first time, seek counseling with your partner. Discuss why it happened and what it means to both of you. This could lead the two of you to be more honest, and perhaps more trusting and intimate.

3 Discuss the seriousness of the affair.

Talk about whether the indiscretion was a one-time incident with someone of little consequence, or whether your partner is in an ongoing relationship. Talk about the difference and think hard about what the circumstances mean to both of you. Professional counseling can help clarify your feelings and priorities. It can also help you to rebuild a trusting relationship, if this is still desired.

4 Decide what you want first—then ask your partner to decide what she wants.

The best possibility is if you both want the same thing, either an end to your relationship or an end to the affair.

5 Act according to your wishes, not your partner's.

If you want to work it out but your partner does not, work on the relationship until you are certain you have tried your best to salvage things. If this is a recurring problem with your partner and you have talked about it at length before, it probably means that she wants out, or that you can expect her to continue having affairs. To end the relationship, go to page page 255.

HOW TO HAVE AN AFFAIR AND NOT GET CAUGHT

1 Assemble an array of convincing alibis and wit-ness-es to explain your frequent disappearances.

Telling your partner "I have to work late" will only get you so far. Enlist the help of a friend or colleague, and have them "invite" you to a reception or sports event, or call with an "emergency." Create a false trail of evidence by having them leave messages on your answering machine that your partner will hear.

2 Do not make multiple, obvious changes to your life-style.

Do not alter the way you dress or the foods you eat all at once. This will tip off your partner that something has changed.

3 Do not discuss topics you previously knew nothing about.

If your lover has encouraged you to become interested in sports or cooking or opera or other topics you never cared about, do not suddenly start talking about them with your partner, who may wonder—or ask—how you knew that.

4 Do not change all your sexual habits at once.

An affair might make you more sexually adventurous,

Always pay cash. Avoid credit cards.

Use cell phones. Never use the hotel phone.

Use room service. Avoid popular restaurants.

Always drive separately. Never drive together.

but do not try too many new things at once with your partner.

5 Never leave for work wearing one outfit and return wearing another.
Keep a change of clothing in your car or at your office and wear that outfit with your lover. Afterward, change back into the clothing you wore when you left home. This will help avoid evidence of your indiscretion (e.g., lipstick, cologne or perfume, or inappropriate wrinkles). Make sure that you do the laundry that contains your "affair" clothing.

6 Take a shower to remove the scent of the affair.
Bathing is especially necessary if you have been in a smoky bar, if your lover wears strong aftershave or perfume, or if you have a dog waiting at home.

7 Never call your partner from a hotel or motel phone, or from a restaurant.
Use your cell phone only—caller ID may reveal your whereabouts.

8 Pay bills in cash only.
Never use a credit card to charge meals, hotels, or day trips. Your partner will probably notice the increase in spending or find the charge slip. Make sure you have enough cash before you head off to your rendezvous; cash machine usage is traceable as well.

9   Drive in a separate car from your lover.

Should there be an accident or a police incident, there will not be any official record of another passenger in the car with you. There will also be no unintentional physical traces—adjusted seat, forgotten scarf—of the passenger.

10   Do not go to fancy or popular restaurants with your lover.

Out-of-the-way places are best; you are less likely to be spotted by friends of your partner. Places just out of town are even better. Room service in a hotel is very private.

IF YOU ARE CAUGHT

1   Do not deny your guilt.

Admit your indiscretion immediately. Dissembling only makes matters worse.

2   Decide immediately whether or not you want to continue the affair.

You will have to be clear about your choice. Ask yourself if you would rather continue with the lover or with your partner. Be honest with yourself and act accordingly.

3   If you want out of your relationship, cut the cord immediately and be ruthless.

Do not try to be nice or understanding—it will only make things more difficult for your soon-to-be-ex-partner. Be a jerk—it will make it easier for them to move on. Explain that you have simply fallen for someone else, that you can't help it, and that you realize that your relationship must end.

4 | If you want to continue your relationship, be prepared to work hard.
Regaining trust will be a long haul. Proceed to steps 5 through 7.

5 | Be completely honest with your partner.
Answer all questions and admit your wrongdoing fully. Constantly reiterate how much you care for your partner. Your steadfastness and honesty is your only hope. Gifts can be an essential part of making up, but mostly you will have to put in a lot of time and energy to make amends.

6 | Do not give up on the relationship.
Prepare yourself for many difficult conversations and arguments. You will have to explain your true intentions time and time again, and it may be a struggle even to begin a conversation at times. Do not take the easy way out. If kicked out of the house, do not leave easily; make it clear that you are willing to struggle through whatever you are faced with to make the relationship work.

7 | Avoid all contact with your former lover and potential lovers.
Never look at or discuss someone of the opposite sex unless specifically asked to do so by your partner—and even then, be cautious.

HOW TO SURVIVE A SEX SCANDAL

1 Circle the family.
Gather your spouse, children, and any other available family members for a photo op showing them standing around you looking proud and trusting. Invite the press to film you at a family picnic or volleyball game. Present yourself as a solid family person whose family members continue to support you.

2 Respond quickly.
If the allegations of sexual impropriety are true and can be proved, apologize and say you have asked your family for forgiveness and they have granted it. Then ask voters for forgiveness. If charges against you are false—or true but cannot be proved—vigorously deny them in front of media cameras and urge reporters to respect you and your family's privacy.

3 Do not lie.
Providing inaccurate accounts of your activities may create a whole new avenue for problems.

4 Move on.
When pressed about the scandal by reporters, say you want to focus on issues that affect the everyday lives of your constituents rather than your personal life. Invite the press along to film you engaging in job-related activities such as talking to voters or signing legisla-

Only appear in wholesome family situations.

tion. Present yourself as someone who is too dedicated to his work to let a personal crisis keep him from going forward with more important matters.

5 | Leave town.
If the scandal persists, arrange travel on official business. Do not allow reporters to go along, and do not give a press conference when you arrive. Be visible and untroubled, but not quotable. If you cut off reporters' access to you, the story may die down.

6 | Take refuge in rehab.
If the furor over the scandal does not dissipate, declare that you have an alcohol or prescription drug dependency that drove you to the impropriety. Then check into a secure and secluded rehabilitation clinic.

7 | Ask for forgiveness.
Upon checking out of the rehab clinic, declare that you are cured and now a far better person who can't wait to get back to working for voters. Ask again for forgiveness and vow to work even harder on important issues.

Be aware
- Outside of England and the United States, sexual dalliances are more casually considered by the public.

HOW TO DEAL WITH A CHILD WALKING IN ON YOU

1 Stop moving.

Cease all sexual activity. Stay still, as hurriedly attempting to clothe yourself, or running from the room, could reveal more sweaty or naughty bits to your visitor.

2 Ask the child to leave.

In an even, steady tone of voice, tell the child to return to his own room, and that you will come and speak to him in a moment. If he remains in the room out of shock or curiosity, cover yourself with a bed sheet or towel and gently escort the child out. Do not show anger or frustration with the child.

3 Close the door.

4 Get dressed.

Remove any costumes or accessories you may have been wearing.

5 Allow your child to ask questions.

Go to the child's room and initiate a conversation in a reassuring tone of voice. Ask, "What did you see?" and "What do you think was going on?" Answer your child's questions, but do not volunteer information that is not requested. If your child chooses not to ask anything, do not press the issue. Say goodnight, but remind him that if he wants to talk about it tomorrow, or later on, it is okay.

6 | Explain your actions honestly but gently.
In answer to your child's questions, explain what mommy and daddy were doing, honestly but not explicitly. You were "hugging and cuddling," or "expressing affection for one another in a physical way." Reassure your child that there was no harm intended.

7 | In the future, have a figurative open door policy.
Tell your child that any time he has questions, he should ask you. When he does, answer calmly and honestly, so he does not come to associate sex with furtiveness and mystery.

8 | In the future, have a literal closed door policy.
Buy a lock for your door, and use it.

HOW TO END A
RELATIONSHIP

1 Get out immediately.

The moment you realize you are in—or starting to get into—a relationship that is not working for you, just say "no."

2 Decide on a mode of communication.

Voicemail, e-mail, or a card may be considered cowardly. However, these options have their advantages, particularly for a short-term relationship. If you are ending a long-term relationship, consider drafting a letter as a way to begin a conversation. Hand it to your partner to read while you are there.

3 Be kind.

Mention the things you like about your partner and express gratitude for the good times you have had together. This may seem contrived, but do it anyway.

4 State your position simply.

Be decisive, leaving no room for doubt or negotiation. It is not necessary for the other person to agree with you or to understand your reasons, but try to explain. One of the consequences of terminating a relationship is that you no longer have to get the other person to understand or agree.

5 | Keep the focus on yourself.
Talk only about yourself, not the other person: Don't make it their fault. Say something simple and true, such as, "I prefer not to continue dating, but I want you to know how much I have enjoyed your sense of humor," or, "This relationship just is not working for me." If necessary, repeat these phrases.

6 | Do not belabor the point.
You do not need to go over all the advantages and disadvantages of the relationship. Do not offer critical feedback or long explanations. If your real reason for breaking up might be painful for the other person to hear, do not mention it.

7 | Do not try to take away the pain.
You are doing what is right for you and the other person has a right to a response. It is no longer your job to make the person feel better. Be firm but not cruel.

8 | Never say, "I will call you."
When tossed out insincerely, this phrase is unimaginative and unkind. Instead, try saying something more honest and more final: "Maybe we will see each other again sometime. If not, have a nice life."

HOW TO STOP A WEDDING

If the object of your affection is about to marry someone else, you need to act quickly to present your case
or forever hold your peace.

1 Make your feelings known before the service.
If you cannot appeal directly to the bride (or groom),
ask to speak to the officiant. The officiant should be
trained in how to handle such situations (go to step 4).

2 If you cannot stop the ceremony beforehand, wait
until the ceremony.
When you hear the officiant ask, "Does anyone know
a reason why these two people should not wed?" stand
up, say "I do," and approach the wedding party. (If you
do not wish to speak out, proceed to step 5.)

3 Ask the officiant if you can present your concerns in
private.

4 Present your objections.
The bride and groom will most likely join you and the
officiant for a consultation. If all agree with you (very
unlikely), the wedding will be halted. If the service is
to continue, respect the decision and leave immediately. Expect to be escorted from the premises.

Feigning a seizure will stop the ceremony.

5 If you do not have the courage to speak up during the ceremony, feign illness.

Fainting is a common occurrence at weddings, and faking it may not stop the ceremony. Instead, feign a seizure. Be sure to act before the vows are spoken. During the commotion while you are being carried out, insist on speaking with the officiant and then confess your feelings.

6 Pull the fire alarm.

If you cannot fake illness, pull the fire alarm. This will disrupt the ceremony, but will only delay the service until the alarm can be turned off. Use this time to speak with the officiant.

7 | If the ceremony has been completed, prevent the signing of the wedding license.

This is your last chance to prevent the marriage. Exchanging vows may make the marriage legitimate in the eyes of most people, but not necessarily in the eyes of the law. All states require a certificate of marriage signed by the officiant, bride, and groom. Traditionally, this document is not signed until after the service. Immediately after the ceremony, speak to the officiant and try to prevent the signing.

8 | If the license has been signed, try to prevent the marriage from being consummated.

In some states and in some religions, the marriage is not final until physical consummation. Find out where the bride and groom are planning to spend the first night and profess your love one last time. If that fails, your only hope is divorce.

IT'S OVER
(LET'S BE FRIENDS)

HOW TO CONFRONT A CHEATING PARTNER

1 Get the facts.
Obtain inarguable documentation such as photographs, copies of emails, recordings, and sworn statements.

2 Meet on your own turf.
Make accusations of infidelity in person. Choose a location where you feel comfortable. Avoid public places, in case either of you starts to cry or yell.

3 State your case.
Frighten and confuse him by disclosing what you know in a calm way. Produce the evidence. Maintain the clinical composure of a doctor giving blood test results.

4 Listen to his explanation.
Wait until he finishes and evaluate the degree of honesty.

5 Tell him you need time.
Say that you need time to think about his transgression, even if you have no intention of staying with him.

6 Dump him.
Wait two days and break up via text message or voicemail.

Throw your drink at your best friend.

how to confront a cheating partner

How to Respond When Your Girl-friend Cheats with Your Best Friend

1 Invite your closest friends—including your girlfriend and your best friend—to dinner at an expensive restaurant.

2 Toast your friends.
After dinner, but before the bill arrives, raise your glass and make a sentimental toast to all your friends. Mention how grateful you are to have such wonderful, true friends.

3 Out the cheaters.
End the speech by announcing to everyone that your girlfriend and your best friend are sleeping with each other behind your back. Hold up photos. Read aloud from printed e-mails.

4 Throw your drink at your best friend.

5 Exit the restaurant.
Leave before the bill arrives.

INSTANT SOLUTION

SPOT CHECK FOR CHEATERS

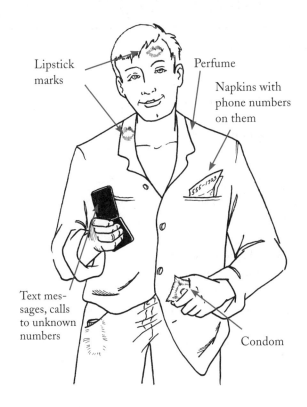

Lipstick marks

Perfume

Napkins with phone numbers on them

Text messages, calls to unknown numbers

Condom

Look for telltale signs of cheating.

HOW TO LIVE WITH AN EX UNTIL ONE OF YOU MOVES OUT

✪ Divide the apartment.
Affix tape to the floor. Move all belongings to appropriate side. Hang drapes or sheets around your space to create the feeling of separate rooms.

✪ Arrange a board in the center of the bed.
Divide pillows evenly.

✪ Label food.
Declare certain cabinets off-limits. Claim sides of the refrigerator.

✪ Cut your couple pictures in half.
Return to appropriate parties.

✪ Divvy up antidepressants in the medicine cabinet.

✪ Schedule custody of the shared pet.
Draw up a timetable that clearly outlines when each of you is allotted time with Spot.

✪ Arrange for two entrances.
Take turns entering and exiting the apartment through the fire escape.

✪ Communicate via sticky notes.

chapter 6: it's over

Divide the apartment to create the feeling of separate rooms.

HOW TO DEAL WITH BEING LEFT AT THE ALTAR

✪ Remain calm.

✪ Go to the reception.
Immediately move on to the reception area.

✪ Celebrate.
Open the Champagne and party. You have dodged years of pain and misery, and probably divorce.

✪ Turn the wedding toast into a wedding roast.
Make jokes at the absent groom's expense. Invite the guests to join in.

✪ Find someone who is single at the reception.
Hook up.

✪ Throw the wedding dress.
Toss the wedding dress into the crowd instead of the bouquet.

Be Aware
• A wedding insurance policy won't cover a change of heart or cold feet.

Toss the wedding dress instead of the bouquet.

WORST BREAKUP LINES

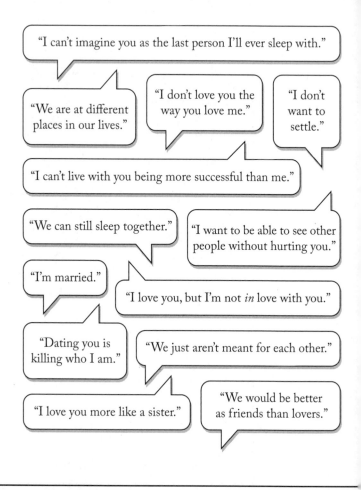

"I can't imagine you as the last person I'll ever sleep with."

"We are at different places in our lives."

"I don't love you the way you love me."

"I don't want to settle."

"I can't live with you being more successful than me."

"We can still sleep together."

"I want to be able to see other people without hurting you."

"I'm married."

"I love you, but I'm not *in* love with you."

"Dating you is killing who I am."

"We just aren't meant for each other."

"I love you more like a sister."

"We would be better as friends than lovers."

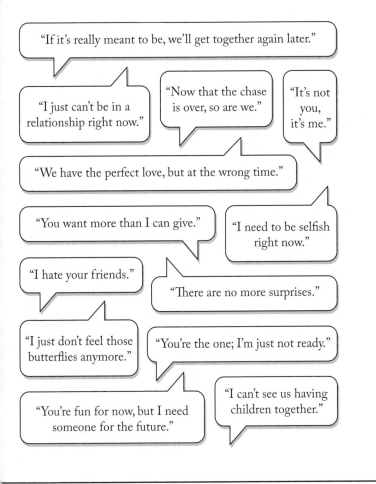

"If it's really meant to be, we'll get together again later."

"I just can't be in a relationship right now."

"Now that the chase is over, so are we."

"It's not you, it's me."

"We have the perfect love, but at the wrong time."

"You want more than I can give."

"I need to be selfish right now."

"I hate your friends."

"There are no more surprises."

"I just don't feel those butterflies anymore."

"You're the one; I'm just not ready."

"You're fun for now, but I need someone for the future."

"I can't see us having children together."

Signs You're Having Breakup Sex

- One of you is crying.

- Both of you are crying.

- You stop to take a phone call.

- You're watching TV.

- You're thinking about shopping.

- You're both fully clothed.

- You don't like the way they smell.

- The lights are on.

- You shake hands afterward.

- The sex has taken on a renewed vigor.

HOW TO BREAK UP
WITH YOUR BOSS

1 Set up a meeting with your boss.
Schedule the meeting on Friday. Ask him to meet you for lunch. Pick a spot where business lunches are taken.

2 Prepare an agenda.
Include a presentation of the reasons why you wish to end the relationship with your boss. Include visual aids.

3 Take the blame.
Whatever the real reason for the breakup, blame yourself. Go over the list of all the things that attracted you to him in the first place, but then emphasize a much longer list of reasons not to continue. Point out that risking your professional career—or his—is not worth it.

4 Agree on containment.
Make it clear that your affair—and now the breakup—are personal matters between the two of you, and that office gossip would be detrimental to the both of you.

5 Act professional.
End on the positive message that you are both smart, responsible, and professional and can take this result in stride.

Give a presentation on the reasons why you wish to end the relationship. Include visual aids.

Be Aware

- Shred the agenda and presentation materials after the meeting.

BREAKUP TEXTS

- 4GET IT

- TTYN

- C U NVR

- ITS OVR

- H8 U, MOVD ON

- UR DUMPT

- U & I R DUN

- NO LUV U NO MO

- BEAT IT

- U SUK

- U R NOW EX

Signs You're Not Over Your Ex

- You accidentally call anyone you are dating by your ex's name.

- Your new relationship is with your old "safety."

- You call your ex's roommate regularly.

- You make lunch dates with your ex's mother.

- You sob uncontrollably when you hear "your song."

- Your social networking status is still "taken."

- You call her when you're drunk.

- You call her when you're sober.

- You check her online photo-sharing account hourly for updates.

- You are still planning the wedding.

- You sleep with her picture.

- You are parked outside of her house.

THINGS BACHELORS DON'T HAVE TO DO

- Buy vegetables
- Vacuum
- Buy anything "lite"
- Buy wine coolers
- Drink diet soda
- Stock the freezer with frozen yogurt
- Watch sports on mute
- Put down the toilet seat
- Hang up towels
- Do laundry
- Wipe hair out of the sink
- Belch quietly
- Clean
- Eat at the kitchen table
- Make the bed
- Watch the *Lifetime* channel
- Drink out of glasses
- Host dinner parties
- Get out of bed before noon

Instant Solution

Spot a Liar

Lack of eye contact

Flared nostrils

Excessive sweating

Hand to face touching

Look for telltale signs of lying.

THE 6 INGREDIENTS OF A
BREAKUP E-MAIL

1. **Vagueness:** Give nonspecific reasons why you are unable to be in a relationship (e.g., you need space, the timing isn't right, or you have mental problems you need to sort out.)

2. **Diplomacy:** Include a sentence about how much you will always treasure the time you had with each other.

3. **A compliment:** Mention something nice or unique about her. If nothing comes to mind, offer an unspecific compliment ("You're such a special person.").

4. **Well-wishing:** Offer a sincere-sounding sentiment wishing her well in the future.

5. **A firm goodbye:** Avoid open-ended statements or questions that might invite a reply—unless she has some of your stuff. In that case, offer a firm breakup and a firm plan to retrieve your belongings.

6. **Cute emoticon:** End with a ????.

the 6 ingredients of a breakup e-mail

HOW TO STEAL YOUR STUFF BACK

⭐ Use a duplicate key to get in her apartment.
Tell her you want to meet at a restaurant to talk. Go to her apartment instead. Unlock the door with the copy of her house key that she gave you and gather your belongings while she is waiting for you at the restaurant.

⭐ Climb the fire escape.
Enter through a window. Ensure that your ex is not home at the time.

⭐ Drill the lock open.
Mess up the apartment to create the appearance of a burglary.

⭐ Tell your ex's landlord that you want to surprise her.
Ask him to let you in her apartment. Explain that you are planning to cook her a romantic dinner for when she gets home from work. Bring roses as a prop.

⭐ Enlist a third party to stop by for a "visit."
Give her a duffle bag and a detailed list of your belongings that need to be retrieved while ostensibly on a social visit. Pay this person if necessary.

Use the fire escape to enter and exit your ex's apartment.

CHECKLIST FOR GETTING

STOP

- Brushing your teeth
- Showering
- Shaving
- Using deodorant
- Changing your clothes
- Working out
- Sharing the covers
- Flushing
- Having sex
- Calling
- Asking questions
- Answering questions
- Inviting her to do anything
- Accompanying her to family/work functions
- Calling her by name
- Complimenting her
- Paying attention to her
- Coming home at night

HER TO BREAK UP WITH YOU

START

- Snoring
- Chewing with your mouth open
- Yodeling
- Leaving the toilet seat up
- Expressing annoyance about her family and friends
- Hitting on her friends
- Hitting on her sister
- Criticizing her appearance
- Breaking her most treasured possessions
- Deleting messages
- Telling her you're not "marriage material"
- Spending all night in Internet chat rooms
- Forgetting her birthday, Valentine's Day, your anniversary
- Scheduling "boys nights" four nights a week
- Talking about the great women you're meeting
- Bringing home dates

CHAPTER 7

WALLOWING

HOW TO TREAT RED, PUFFY EYES

✪ Splash ice-cold water on your face.

✪ Apply a cold compress.
Place a chilled wet washcloth, cucumber slices, metal spoons, or moistened tea bags over your eyes for ten minutes. Herbal teas such as chamomile are soothing; caffeinated teas restrict blood vessels and reduce swelling.

✪ Hydrate.
Drink plenty of water to avoid inflammation.

✪ Make an egg-white mask.
Beat two egg whites in a bowl and add a few drops of witch hazel. Apply the skin-tightening mixture to the entire face and wait 15 minutes for the mask to dry. Follow up with a light moisturizer.

✪ Exercise.
Jump up and down and swing your arms back and forth to stimulate the lymphatic system, which is responsible for fluid circulation. Sustained exercise will elevate your pulse, increase blood flow, and relax the mind.

✪ Apply hemorrhoid cream.
Hemorrhoid cream constricts blood vessels and reduces inflammation. Squeeze out a pea-sized amount of

cream and spread evenly on the skin around the eyes. Avoid contact with eyes.

✪ Sleep in an upright position.
Lie on your back with your head propped in a vertical position so that gravity pulls the fluid downward. Get comfortable so you can stay in that position most of the night.

✪ Wear makeup.
Cover redness around your eyes with concealer that is a shade lighter than your skin. Mask eyes with shadow, eyeliner, and mascara. Curl your eyelashes to make your eyes look bigger.

✪ Create a cosmetic distraction.
Add a large beauty mark or scar elsewhere on your face.

✪ Style your hair.
Comb your bangs down over your eyes or create a radical hairstyle.

✪ Wear sunglasses.

Create a radical, new hairstyle.

How to Cry in Public

⭐ Breathe.
Take long, slow deep breaths, drawing air in quietly through your nose. Oxygenating the brain is calming.

⭐ Fake a sneeze.
Claim sickness or allergies.

⭐ Pretend to read something funny.
Occupy yourself with a newspaper or book. Force "ha" sounds, timed with your sobs, to disguise your sorrow as laughter.

⭐ Hide.
Stand behind trees or facing a wall to keep your face and tears hidden from view.

⭐ Carry a parasol.
Open an umbrella at the onset of a crying jag, holding it low to cover your eyes.

⭐ Smile.
Confuse your nervous system, and any nearby observers, by sending an opposing signal of happiness.

how to treat red, puffy eyes

BREAKUP FOOD SERVINGS	
BEFORE THE BREAKUP	**AFTER THE BREAKUP**
Gallon of ice cream	Popsicle
Half pint of cream	Creamer packet
Dinner, appetizer, dessert	Half-dish
Pot of coffee	Cup of instant coffee
Half gallon of orange juice	Juice box
Whole rotisserie chicken	Chicken nuggets

SIGNS YOUR NEW PARTNER IS ON THE REBOUND

- He suggests you change your hair color.
- He wants you to wear the new perfume he gave you.
- He asks you to wear his ex's old clothes.
- He calls you by the wrong name.
- He won't let you see the photos he keeps in his wallet.
- He cancels dates with you to hang out with his ex.
- He mentions vacations "we" went on to places you've never been.
- He insists on reading his old love letters to you.

INSTANT SOLUTION

THINGS YOU CAN DO WITH A TATTOO OF YOUR EX'S NAME

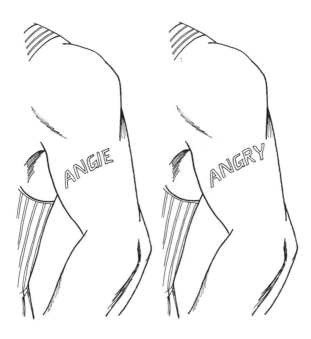

Create a new word out of it.

HOW NOT TO DRINK ALONE

✪   Clink your glass against the fish tank.

✪   Refill the dog's water bowl.
Say "Another round?"

✪   Crash an event.
Find a bar mitzvah, graduation, confirmation, or wedding and join the party.

✪   Frequent the all-night laundromat.
Bring a bottle of wine and glasses.

✪   Carry a flask on the subway.
Do not get off until you have emptied it.

✪   Schedule a hair salon appointment.
Arrive early with a shaker and cups.

Bring a bottle of wine and glasses to the laundromat.

Hangover Remedies

- A pint of beer and a bowl of salty ceviche
- A bacon, egg, and cheese sandwich, with a cola drink
- A plate of burnt toast
- Two liters of Pedialyte or Gatorade
- Ginger
- Bloody Mary
- Two liters of coconut water
- A quick-absorbing painkiller dissolved in carbonated water
- Orange juice
- Black coffee
- Banana
- Applesauce

HOW TO SABOTAGE YOUR EX'S NEW RELATIONSHIP

★ Return clothing.
Send underwear or clothing that she left behind or new clothing that is simply her size, and include a note on the box that says: "You left this last night." Use a messenger and time the delivery for when your ex's new boyfriend will be around.

★ Create a fake e-mail account.
Send an email to your ex's new boyfriend, signed with a fictitious name, claiming that your ex is cheating on him with you, and that you are coming forward because you "feel guilty." Warn that if your ex is confronted, she will deny knowing you.

★ Send photos to her new boyfriend's phone.
Block Caller ID by dialing *76 before his number. Send altered but plausible photos of her with another guy.

★ Be seen with a sexy new girlfriend.
Borrow someone, if necessary.

★ Start a rumor.
Have friends spread the word that you have fallen head over heels for someone she dislikes or views as a threat.

Send your ex intimate apparel with a suggestive note.

⭐ Encourage other guys to make passes at her.
Register her with multiple online dating sites. List her
new boyfriend's e-mail as contact information.

Be Aware
- Cover your tracks since any attempt to sour her new
  relationship will be linked to you.

WHO TO TALK TO IF YOU ARE LONELY

- Telephone operators
- Customer service representatives
- Toll collectors
- Drycleaners
- Bus drivers
- Mail carriers
- Squirrels
- Psychics
- Homeless people
- Cab drivers
- Supermarket clerks
- People sitting next to you on the bus
- People standing behind you in line for a movie
- People on screen during the movie

HOW TO CAMOUFLAGE YOURSELF OUTSIDE OF YOUR EX'S HOME

In Plain View

✪ Adopt a disguise.
Dress as a landscaper, painter, delivery person, road crew worker, or employee of a local utility company. Wear a wig, a hat, and an official-looking uniform.

✪ Look busy.
Use props such as a ladder, lawn mower, clipboard, road cones, or stack of pizza boxes to appear engaged in some activity in a slow, protracted manner allowing for extended surveillance.

✪ Avoid conversations.
If you must talk, use an accent.

✪ Befriend the neighbors.
Make friends with whichever neighbors will give you the most advantageous view of your ex's home when visiting.

Adopt a disguise. Use props.

Out of Sight

⭐ Hide behind shrubbery.
Wear black clothing at night. Dress warmly.

⭐ Climb a tree.

⭐ Park across the street in a car or van.
Change vehicles every day.

INSTANT SOLUTION

MAKE A VOODOO DOLL

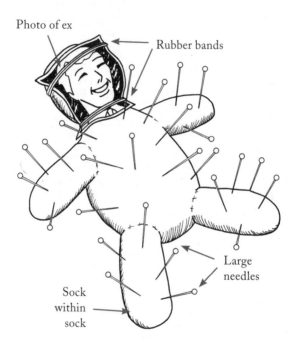

Place needles strategically.

Most Common, But Useless, Breakup Advice

- "Everything happens for a reason."
- "If it was meant to be, you will get back together again."
- "Now you can devote time to your relationship with yourself."
- "You're not a spring chicken anymore; you should get back out there."
- "You can find better."
- "It's better to have loved and lost than not to have loved at all."
- "You're better off without him."
- "Now you can find someone who deserves you."
- "Time heals."
- "It's called a breakup because it was broken."
- "There are plenty of fish in the sea."

CHAPTER 8

MOVING ON

PERSONALITY TYPES TO AVOID	
TYPE	SIGNS
The Mama's Boy	Calls mom on cell phone to ask what to order in restaurants; wears a locket around his neck with her photo
The Freeloader	Has managed to avoid paying for anything since your first date; has somehow moved into your apartment but you can't remember how or when
The Co-Dependent	Blames intractable personal problems on you; encourages you to develop/enjoy these same problems yourself
The Narcissist	Gives you a gift of mirrored sunglasses so he can check himself out while on dates with you
The Playboy	You can taste his cologne from five feet away; speaks French extraneously; not sure he gave you his real name

HOW TO DANCE ON A BAR

1 Find a crowded bar with music playing.
Seek out a bar with an inebriated, appreciative crowd, a laid back bar staff, and a jukebox full of good tunes.

2 Drink the right amount of alcohol.
Imbibe enough so that your inhibitions shrink, but not so much that you cannot climb up and stay on the bar without falling.

3 Dry off the bar where you intend to dance.
Use napkins or a dry bar rag to dry the bar and prevent slipping.

4 Wait for a song you genuinely like.
Load the jukebox upon your arrival to ensure that you will hear music that excites you. Choose upbeat songs that you know how to dance to.

5 Enlist two people to help you up onto the bar.
Place a hand on each of their shoulders.

6 Prop the knee of your dominant leg on the bar stool.
If the stool swivels, instruct your helpers to hold it still.

Dance, keeping foot movements to a minimum.

7 | Hold your supporters' hands.
Remove your hands from their shoulders and grab their hands.

8 | Swing your nondominant leg onto the bar.
Continue to hold their hands until you find your balance.

9 | Dance.
Keep foot movements to a minimum.

10 | Sing along.
Lip-sync if you do not have a great voice.

11 | Smile.
Enjoy yourself.

12 | Take a bow when the song is over.
Do not overstay your welcome.

13 | Grasp your supporters' hands and step down from the bar.
Do not "stage dive" into the audience.

Be Aware

* Be mindful of your short skirt when climbing onto the bar.

Places NOT to Dance on a Bar

- Country clubs

- Funerals

- Bars where there are no other women

- Bars where the other women aren't wearing any clothes

- Events where a makeshift bar is set up

- A happy hour with your boss or your direct reports

Instant Solution

Make Your Bed Feel Fuller

Add pillows, comforters, and stuffed animals to your bed.
Place a body-sized pillow, or a television, in the spot
where your partner used to sleep.

HOW TO MAKE YOUR ONLINE PROFILE MORE ALLURING

1 | Post a flattering photograph.
Pose with children or animals if you are male. Look like you are having the time of your life if you are female.

2 | Use euphemisms.
For instance, avoid the word "unemployed" by saying that you are currently enjoying a sweat-free lifestyle while you search for a new challenge.

3 | Seem rich.
Refer to signs of affluence such as luxury brands, cruises, extended vacations, resorts in exotic locales, and tax shelters.

4 | Seem interesting.
Discuss a variety of interesting hobbies such as rock climbing, photography, and wine.

5 | Seem cultured.
List "favorites" that present you as educated and sophisticated, yet not pretentious. Mention highbrow and mainstream books, movies, TV shows, and musicians to create the impression that you have ecclectic and wide-ranging taste.

*Post a flattering photograph. Pose with children
or animals if you are male.*

6 Keep it positive.
Avoid mention of your breakup.

PERSONAL AD PHOTO DECODER	
PHOTO POSTED FOR ONLINE PERSONAL AD	**WHAT IT SAYS ABOUT YOU**
Photos with an ex-boyfriend or girlfriend	I have been on a date before.
High school yearbook photos	I am 20 pounds heavier than this.
Party photos	I am drunk right now.
Baby photo	I was cute a long time ago.
Arrest "mug" shots	I will stalk you if we break up.
You with stuffed animals	I will stalk you if we break up.
Altered pictures of you with celebrities	I live in my parents' basement.
Wedding photos	I am married.
Nude photos	I am desperate.

HOW TO DEAL WITH SEEING YOUR EX FOR THE FIRST TIME AFTER THE BREAKUP

1 Do not run away.
You will have to see your ex eventually so it is best to deal with it now and get it over with.

2 Do not reach for a drink.
Alcohol may unleash a wave of emotions.

3 Do not hide behind a potted plant.
He will see you.

4 Do not avoid eye contact.
When your ex spots you, do not avert your eyes. Smile and wave.

5 Approach your ex.
Assume an air of purposeful nonchalance.

6 Greet your ex warmly, but not too warmly.
Pretend you are greeting an old friend from elementary school.

7 Remain standing.
Do not sit down or get trapped in a group with your ex.

Do not hide.

8 | Ask specific but neutral questions.
Only ask questions that you are sure he will not respond to with devastating information. General inquiries such as "How are you," may result in an upsetting update on his love life, while asking if he ever took that trip to Hawaii may risk the response, "Yes, on my honeymoon."

9 | Cultivate an air of mystery.
Give an upbeat but vague account of your life since you last saw each other. Offer that "things" have been "great" and that you have been "busy." Let him wonder.

10 | Move on.
Limit the conversation to no more than five minutes. Excuse yourself, saying you have to get back to your companion(s)—even if you are alone. Say it's been great running into him.

11 | Do not look back.
Walk away slowly and confidently.

TURN YOUR APARTMENT BACK INTO A BACHELOR PAD	
OUT	**IN**
Photos of you with your ex	Photos of your dog
Bubble bath	Athlete's foot powder
Accent pillows	Takeout menus
Scented candles	Ashtray
Skim milk	Beer
Romantic comedies	Action films
Yoga mat	Bench press
Clothing catalogs	Car magazines
Wine coolers	Beer
Vanity mirror	Flat screen TV

INSTANT SOLUTION

EATING OUT ALONE

Bring a pet and a good book.

HOW TO TREAT A GYM ADDICTION

1 Examine your behavior.
- Do you work out multiple times a day?
- Do you show up at the gym when you know it is not open?
- Do fellow gym-goers think you are an employee of the gym?
- Have you ever lied to family members or friends about the amount of time you spend at the gym?
- Do you have designated equipment that no one else is allowed to use?
- Do you consistently and repeatedly exceed the time limit on the treadmill?
- Does the thought of your gym closing for a holiday terrify you?

2 Admit that you have a problem and that you need help.
Realize that you are not responsible for your disease—but you are responsible for your recovery. Make recovery a priority.

3 Admit to one other person that you have a problem.
This person will help you wean yourself off the gym.
This person should not work at the gym.

Admit that you have a problem.

319. how to treat a gym addiction

4 Reduce the amount of time you spend at the gym.
Replace your gym time with other activities to take your mind off the withdrawal you may experience. Make it a point to engage in activities that do not involve exercise. Read a magazine, go to the movies, or take a nap.

5 Watch yourself carefully and be willing to forgive a relapse.
Be prepared to relapse, which is a common occurrence on the road to recovery. If you fall back into your old gym habits, admit it to yourself and seek out others for support.

6 Do not be afraid to ask for help when you need it.
Consult a therapist. Form a support group for other exercise addicts.

7 Remember that no one is perfect.
Seek the ability to change the things you can, and to accept the things you cannot change.

Be Aware
- Replacing gym habits with workouts at home is a sign of addiction, not a step to recovery.

INSTANT SOLUTION

RESTOCK THE FRIDGE

Fill your refrigerator with the essentials.

Divorce Rates by Country
Percent of Marriages that End in Divorce

Top 5		Bottom 5	
Sweden	54.9%	Turkey	6.0%
United States	54.8%	Bosnia and Herzegovina	5.0%
Belarus	52.9%	Republic of Macedonia	5.0%
Finland	51.2%	Sri Lanka	1.5%
Luxembourg	47.4%	India	1.1%

HOW TO REGAIN
YOUR CONFIDENCE

1 Hang a small mirror in a location you walk past often.
Post affirmations such as "I am special," "I am unique," or "I am the best me I can be," around the mirror. Every time you walk past the mirror, smile at your reflection and recite the affirmations out loud.

2 Write down compliments you receive.
Place them in a jar. The next time you are feeling worthless, take out a compliment and read it aloud.

3 Call your mother.
Tell her you are feeling down in the dumps.

4 Adopt a mantra.
Recite a positive mantra to yourself every morning before you begin your day.

5 Strut past a construction site.
Put on a skirt or dress and high heels. Apply red lipstick. Style your hair. Choose a heavily trafficked construction site to walk past. Sway your hips. Smile. Stop and ask the workers for directions.

6 Make a list of all the people who have ever had a crush on you.

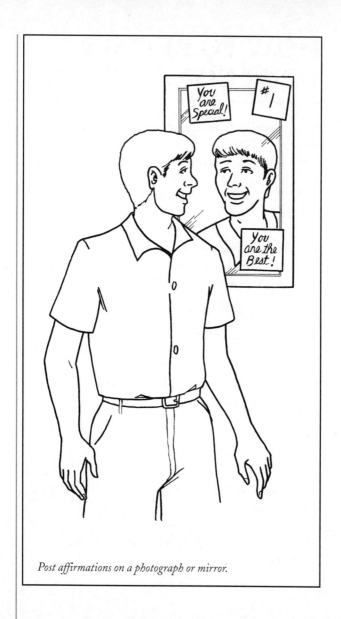

Post affirmations on a photograph or mirror.

7 Exercise.
Release endorphins and boost your mood by exercising for at least 20 minutes every day.

8 Eat spicy food.
Hot foods also release endorphins.

9 Join a group or club.
Surround yourself with positive people who enjoy doing similar activities. Open yourself up to meeting new people.

10 Volunteer.
Helping out others who may be in difficult situations themselves will provide perspective on your situation. It can be reassuring to see people worse off than you are.

11 Try a new hobby.
Plant a garden, learn a new language, go skydiving, or learn how to play the guitar.

12 Get glamorous.
Have your hair, makeup, and nails done. Accentuate a favorite feature. Have professional photographs taken.

CHAPTER 9

TYING THE KNOT

HOW TO RAISE
MONEY FOR THE
WEDDING

⭐ **Ask family members to pay for specific expenses.**
Have numbers ready to justify costs. If you sense resistance, threaten to elope or to have the reception at a seedy nightclub. For grandparents, offer upgrades at the reception in exchange for funding, such as seating at a table far from the band, their food served first, or wider, cushioned seats.

⭐ **Register for wedding ceremony and reception components.**
Instead of a bridal registry for china, crystal, and silver, register for floral arrangements, the band, limousine service, liquor for the reception, and each course of the meal.

⭐ **Hold a raffle.**
Offer the guests a chance to buy tickets to win the wedding dress, a ride in the limo, or a chance to join the honeymoon.

⭐ **Wash guests' cars.**
Hire a student at a low hourly rate to sell expensive car washes to the guests as they attend the ceremony and reception.

Procure sponsors to help defray costs.

✪ Sell your belongings on Internet auction sites.
Check to see which items you've registered for have been bought, or estimate which items you are sure to receive, and sell them online. The buyer will send payment, and, after the wedding, you send the sold item.

✪ Procure sponsors.
Strike a deal with a local company. Agree to place its logo on the invitation, wedding dress, tuxedo, or cake. Have the band leader announce each song with, "This song has been brought to you by the good people at [name of company]." Hang company banners around the altar and behind the bandstand. Allow the company to set up a kiosk at the ceremony and reception site to dispense information, key chains, and other swag.

✪ Sell incentive packages to investors.
Offer a percentage of wedding gifts, naming rights to kids, occasional dinners at your home, an invitation to the wedding (with preferred seating), the first dance with the bride/groom, and, for enough money, the opportunity to give away the bride.

HOW TO MAKE YOUR BETROTHED'S PARENTS LIKE YOU

⭐ Be direct.
Have a conversation about your feelings. Start with, "I've noticed a change in our relationship, and I was wondering if I have done something to offend." Talk about the issue from your point of view. Use phrases such as "I feel this" as opposed to "you did this" so they will not feel attacked. Listen carefully and remain open to criticism.

⭐ Be nice.
Remain pleasant and respectful, and you will eventually wear them down. Be patient, as this might take some time.

⭐ Arrange for testimonials.
Ask friends, relatives, and neighbors to vouch for your value as a human being when your future in-laws come to visit. Leave information packets on their pillows that include letters of recommendation from coaches, employers, teachers, and religious and community leaders. Include a pie chart that expresses the amount of time you devote each day to your future spouse.

✪ Volunteer your services.

Help with household tasks such as changing the kitty litter, caulking the tub, or walking the dog at the crack of dawn. Take them to the airport at rush hour, teach your betrothed's younger siblings how to drive, install their new computer system, re-point the brick exterior of their home, prepare their tax returns, refinish the floors throughout their house, and detail their car.

✪ Find a common bond.

If your in-laws dislike you because they do not know you, invite them out together or separately on outings they enjoy. If your mother-in-law likes tea, ask her to tea. If she prefers the theater, take her to a play. Take your father-in-law golfing, or if he's a man of few words, to the movies or a nightclub. Pick up the tab.

✪ Plant a diary where your in-laws will be sure to find it.

Fill the diary with virtuous thoughts and aspirations. Declare your love for your betrothed repeatedly. Add entries about how much you like your future in-laws and how much you hope they'll like you, too.

✪ Pretend you are friends with celebrities.

Find out who their heroes are (politicians, authors, activists, sports figures, movie stars, etc.) and autograph and frame a glossy photo of a celebrity to yourself. Mention to your future in-laws you might be able to pull a few strings if they'd like to meet the famous person.

✪ Pay for the wedding.
If you or your family are already paying for the wedding, offer to pay off their mortgage or car payments.

✪ Let them move in.
Give them the big bathroom.

✪ Promise to provide them with a grandchild within a negotiated period of time.

HOW TO SURVIVE THE BACHELOR PARTY

How to Smoke a Cigar

1 Clip the head.
The head, or smoking end, of the cigar is covered by a small area of leaf called the cap. Using a sharp cigar cutter, quickly make a guillotine cut, removing a small section ($^1/_4$ inch or less) of the cap. Do not cut below the end of the cap, or the wrapper may come apart. If no cigar cutter is available, punch a hole in the cap using the tip of a pen or pencil.

2 Hold the cigar in your nondominant hand.

3 Ignite a torch lighter or a long wooden match.
Do not put the cigar to your lips.

4 Toast the end.
Carefully move the flame to the foot (end) while rotating the cigar slowly. This will ensure an even burn. The foot should ignite thoroughly and evenly.

5 When the foot is lit, bring the cigar to your lips.

6 Draw smoke into your mouth.
Suck the smoke through the cigar slowly and evenly

while still holding the flame an inch or two from the foot.

7 Puff gently until the foot is completely lit.
Do not inhale the smoke into your lungs.

8 Exhale.
Savor the flavor of the cigar in your mouth for a few seconds before expelling the smoke.

9 Repeat steps 7 and 8.
Take one or two draws from the cigar per minute, but do not rush. Rotate the cigar slowly in your fingers or allow it to sit in an ashtray between draws. Keep the foot elevated to maintain an even burn. Avoid squeezing the cigar.

10 Flick the ash.
Allow half an inch to an inch of ash to accumulate on the foot. Tap the cigar gently with a finger to make the ash fall. Many cigar smokers will try to get the ash as long as possible before flicking it. However, you should flick the ash if you feel it is about to fall and burn a hole in clothing or furniture.

11 Extinguish the cigar.
Many smokers will discard a cigar when half to three-quarters has been smoked. A quality cigar may be smoked as long as its flavor is still pleasing and the smoke is cool enough to be comfortable in your mouth.

Be Aware

- A natural—a cigar with a light brown wrapper—is mild and is more appropriate for beginners. (A maduro, or a cigar with a dark brown wrapper, will be rich and full flavored, but may be too harsh for a novice smoker.)
- The wrapper should not be dry, flaking, or crack when handled.
- Gently squeeze the cigar. It should be firm and give lightly to the touch, then regain its shape. A moist cigar has been overhumidified and will not draw well.
- While it may be socially frowned upon, a cigar may be extinguished and relit. Scoop or blow all carbon from the foot of the cigar before relighting, or cut the cigar just above the burned section.

HOW TO SURVIVE A NIGHT IN JAIL

1 Request a single.
If you notice an empty cell, ask to be housed there. Do not offer special reasons for wanting a private cell—those factors may work against you if you are later placed in a group cell.

2 Do not show fear.
Fear means weakness in jail. If you cannot stop shaking, pretend you are psychologically unsound: Wave your arms around, babble nonsense, and yell at no one in particular.

Relax hand and roll finger to make a clean print.

3 | Stay within sight of the guard.
The cell may be monitored in person by a guard or via closed-circuit television. Make sure you remain visible.

4 | Do not sleep.
Lying down on a bench or cot gives other inmates the opportunity to claim that you are lying on "their" bunk. Sit on the floor with your back to the wall, preferably in a corner of the cell. Do not remove any clothing to use as a blanket or pillow, or you will risk losing the item to other inmates.

5 | Keep to yourself.
Do not start a conversation with anyone, but do not be rude. Answer any questions you are asked, and keep your responses short. Do not talk about the reason for your arrest, as there may be police informants in the cell. Do not make eye contact with other inmates, but do not avert your eyes.

6 | Do not accept favors.
Other inmates may offer to help you in various ways, then claim that you "owe" them. Resist the temptation to ask for or accept help.

7 | Do not tell anyone you are a college student.
The population of the cell may make various assumptions about the privileges, wealth, health, preferences, defenselessness, connections, and value of students.

8 | Do not try to escape.

HOW TO SURVIVE THE BRIDAL SHOWER

How to Make a Toilet Paper Dress

Most bridal showers include group games. A game that the bride and her guests are often asked to play involves breaking into groups and dressing several models in toilet paper to see who can create the best bridal gown.

1 Construct the bodice.
- Unwrap a roll of toilet paper around the model's midsection, beginning at her waist and wrapping around her torso, in overlapping layers, until she is wrapped to just underneath her underarms.
- Without detaching the paper, make a small sleeve by wrapping from underneath one of her arms to over and around the opposite shoulder. Repeat over the other shoulder to give the dress a slightly off-the-shoulder neckline.

2 Make the skirt.
- Tape the free end of a fresh roll to the waist on the dress's bodice, unrolling a strip long enough to reach the floor (or your desired length—a short dress can also be nice, especially if your model is wearing a mini skirt or shorts).

- Tape the next piece to the waist of the dress, over-lapping to about the middle of the first strip. Unroll to meet the length of the first strip.
- Repeat in this way until you've taped strips the whole way around the model's waist.
- A staggered effect, with strips of different lengths, can earn extra points for creativity.

3 Make a belt.
Unroll several layers of toilet paper directly around the model's waist, to cover the area where the skirt is taped to the bodice of the dress.

4 Make the veil.
- Unwrap about four feet of toilet paper.
- Fold it in half, so that it's two feet long, and then in half again.
- Now fold it lengthwise several times, until you have a fairly sturdy, thick strip to use as a headband. Tape the sides of the headband to secure it.
- Tape several three- to five-foot-long strips of toilet paper to the headband. The length of the strips can be adjusted to suit your preference.
- Use bobby pins to secure the veil to the model's head.

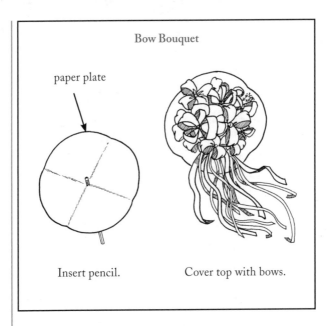

Bow Bouquet

paper plate

Insert pencil.

Cover top with bows.

How to Make a Bow Bouquet

As the bride unwraps her presents, a member of the wedding party is responsible for making a bow bouquet for the bride to carry at her wedding rehearsal. You will need a paper plate; a pencil, pen, or other long skinny object; tape; and bows and ribbons from gifts.

1 Make the base.
Fold a paper plate in quarters, then unfold. (The folds in the plate will provide the bow bouquet with volume.) Insert the pencil, pen, or other long skinny object into the center of the plate, push it through so

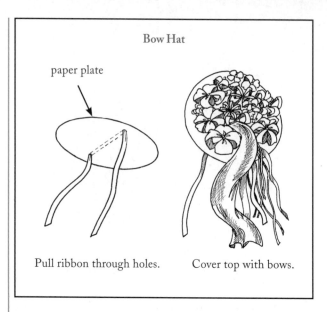

Bow Hat

paper plate

Pull ribbon through holes.   Cover top with bows.

that only about an inch shows through the top, and tape it in place at the top and bottom.

7 | Build the bouquet.
As the bride unwraps her gifts, take each bow and ribbon and tape it on top of the plate. Place smaller bows in the center, and larger bows on the outside. Wrap long, curling ribbons around the pencil, allowing them to hang down from under the plate. If the bride has a lot of presents, layer the bows as necessary. Be sure to use all of the bows and ribbons.

Alternate Method:

In some cases, the bows and ribbons from the bride's gifts are used to make a bow hat rather than a bouquet. To make a bow hat:

- Poke a hole about half an inch from the edge of a paper plate. Repeat on the opposite side.
- Thread a thick, wide ribbon through one of the holes, tying a knot at the end on top of the plate to keep it from slipping out. Repeat on the opposite side, leaving the bottom ends loose to tie the hat to the bride's head.
- Tape bows and ribbons to the top of the paper plate so that the largest bows are around the outside edge, the smallest in the center. Attach all long ribbons to hang down from the back of the hat.
- Tie the hat to the bride's head with the two wide ribbons at the sides. Laugh. Cry.

HOW TO FIX THE BRIDE'S WEDDING ATTIRE

Stained Dress

1 For tea, coffee, or dirt stains.
- Apply a dot of clear liquid soap and water to a cloth and dab gently on the back of the stain. Do not use excessive water. Do not rub the stain, as you will take the finish off the fibers of the dress.
- Dab the cloth with club soda.
- If the stain remains, dab with a solution of white vinegar and water.

2 For a red wine stain.
- Wet a cloth with white wine and blot behind the stain. Do not rub the stain, as you will take the finish off the fibers of the dress.
- When the stain has faded, dab with water to rinse.

3 For grease or makeup stains.
- Gently rub a bit of chalk on the stain to absorb the mark. After a few moments, whisk away the chalk dust.
- If you do not have chalk, try baking soda, baby powder, or talcum powder, but they are less absorbent. Sprinkle powder on and then lightly shake off dress.

Keep the dress off the floor.

4 For a lipstick stain.

- Dab some petroleum jelly on the mark to dissolve the stain.
- If the stain remains, conceal with baby powder, chalk, or baking powder. Blot the stain to remove as much of it as possible. Pat baby powder on the area gently. Also, try rolling a de-linting brush over the stain to lift it off. This works best for stains that are not embedded into the fibers.

Be Aware

- Before treating a stain, read the label on your dress. The fabric will dictate how or if you should clean it. Silk is the most fragile fabric and toughest to clean. Polyester is the easiest.

- White correction fluid or toothpaste may work to cover up a stain, but because they both possess alcohol, they can pull the color out of your dress, leaving a permanent mark even after professional dry cleaning.
- Avoid using hot water, which will set the stain; always use cool or cold water when cleaning.
- After cleaning a stain, dry the area thoroughly. Water marks are a hazard for dresses, particularly silk ones. Use a hair dryer on the coolest setting to dry the area while stretching the fabric with your fingers to prevent wrinkling.

DRESS WET FROM RAIN

1 Do not put the dress in a clothes dryer.
Dryer heat is too intense and can cause the dress to shrink, wrinkle, and lose beading.

2 Air dry.
Air drying is best when there is just a sprinkling of water on the dress and there is no time left before the ceremony. If you have been caught in a downpour, remove the dress and air dry it, then follow up with some hand steaming to remove the resulting wrinkles. If you do not have a hand steamer, hang the dress in the bathroom while running hot water in the shower, creating a makeshift sauna. Another option is to activate the steam component from a clothes iron and wave it near the dress.

3 | Use a hair dryer to dry the dress.
Set the dryer on low and hold it at least 6 inches from the wet fabric. Keep the fabric taut to prevent wrinkling. Use a circular motion with the hair dryer to avoid burning the fabric. Do not try to speed the process by holding the dryer close to the dress; you will only damage the fabric.

4 | Use the hot-air dryer in the bathroom.
Do not let the dress drag on the bathroom floor.

5 | Finish with an iron.
Test the iron first on the inside of the dress. Place a pressing cloth on the dress before applying the iron and keep the setting on low.

Broken Strand of Pearls

1 | Find all the pearls.

2 | Put the pearls on a towel or cloth.
Arrange the pearls so that the biggest pearls are in the middle, flanked by pearls of diminishing size.

3 | Find a needle and string.
Use dental floss, fishing wire, or nylon thread to restring the pearls. Waxed floss is stiff so it will eliminate the need for a needle. Stiffen the end of fishing wire or a thread with glue if you are without a needle.

4 | Make a triple knot on one end of the string.
Add a dab of glue on top of the knot for extra security. Leave extra length on the string beyond the knot for tying.

5 | Add a pearl.

6 | Make a loose overhand knot.
Place a pin, needle, or tweezers in the open knot and slide the knot next to the pearl. Then pull the knot loop snug as you remove the pin, needle, or tweezers.

7 | Add the next pearl.
Keep your knot-tying tension consistent. If time is running out, tie a knot after every five pearls.

8 | Repeat steps 5 through 7 until all the pearls are on the string.
Make a triple knot after the final pearl. Add a dab of glue to the knot.

9 | Tie the necklace on the bride's neck using a secure square knot.
Dab with glue for added strength. Trim off the excess string.

Be Aware

- If the bride's strand of pearls breaks and not enough of the pearls can be located, scan the guests' necks for the best piece of replacement jewelry. Once the most appropriate jewelry has been spotted, ask the guest to help the bride by lending her the jewels for the big event—or at least for the photographs. Most guests will be flattered to help save the day. Be sure to return the jewelry.

BROKEN HEEL

1 Remove both shoes and go barefoot.

Depending on the length of your dress and the formality of your wedding, going barefoot may be an acceptable option. If you are wearing a floor-length gown, you may need to use straight pins to temporarily hem the dress an inch or two at the bottom to keep it from dragging on the floor and tripping you as you walk.

2 Borrow shoes from others.

Ask a member of the wedding party or a guest with the same size foot if you can wear her shoes for the ceremony. Do not be choosy about style or color.

3 Make an emergency heel.

Find a sturdy object or objects the same height as the broken heel. A shot glass, a stack of sticky notes (so long as it's not raining), or a votive candleholder are acceptable choices. Alternatively, use duct tape to

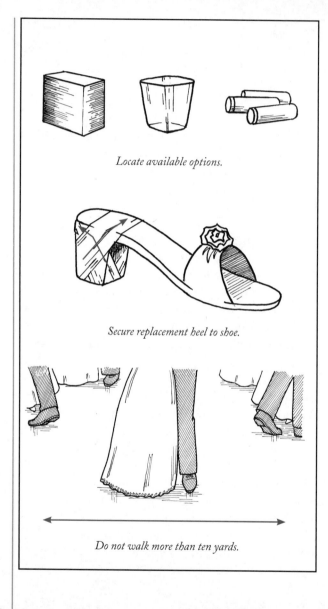

Locate available options.

Secure replacement heel to shoe.

Do not walk more than ten yards.

make a cylinder out of several short pencils or metal lipstick tubes. Wrap duct tape around your shoe and the substitute heel to secure it in place.

Be Aware

- A replacement heel is fine for a short period of light activity, but do not dance, run, carry heavy objects, walk more than 10 yards, or stand for long periods of time with your weight on the emergency heel.

- Once the dancing begins at the reception, your guests will be relieved to see that you have removed your shoes. They will feel much more comfortable about taking off their own uncomfortable and restricting shoes and having fun.

EMERGENCY UP-DO HAIRSTYLE

1 Brush your hair back from your forehead.
Comb it long enough to make the hair on top of your head smooth.

2 Gather your hair at the nape, slightly to the left, as if you were going to put in a low ponytail.

3 Twist the hair twice, in a clockwise direction, to anchor it in place.
You can also use bobby pins to hold the hair in place.

4 Brush the remaining hair down toward the direction of the nape of your neck.

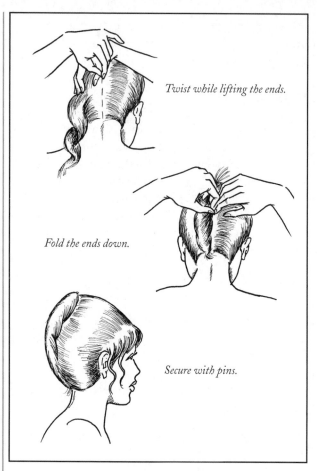

Twist while lifting the ends.

Fold the ends down.

Secure with pins.

5 | Twist it clockwise while lifting the ends.
You are creating a roll effect on the back of your head.

6 | Continue to twist until the roll feels tight and secure.
Your loose ends should be at the top of the roll.

7 With your right hand, fold the ends down toward the nape of your neck, under the twist.

8 Pin the roll in place.
Use your left hand to hold the twist in place while your right hand works the bobby pins. Slide one long pin in the top of the roll, facing down. Place another long pin in the bottom, going up the middle. Insert a final large pin at an angle through the side of the roll. Finish with enough small bobby pins to secure the twist and smooth any ruffled areas.

9 Pull out a few tendrils.
Loosen a few strands of hair around your face for a more romantic look. Curl the strands with a curling iron if one is available.

10 Spray the twist in place with hairspray.

HOW TO FIX THE GROOM'S WEDDING ATTIRE

Tux Too Small

1 Swap tuxedos.
If your tuxedo matches the style of those worn by the groomsmen or waiter, exchange yours for one that fits: It is better for a groomsman or waiter to look poorly dressed than the groom.

2 Expand the waistband.
Make a chain of two or three safety pins, depending on how much additional room is required. Secure the sides of the waistband together using pins. Your cummerbund will hide the fix. Do not remove the cummerbund during the wedding.

3 Replace the pants.
Locate a pair of black pants that fit. Cut a piece of black electrical tape the same length as the pant leg, waist to hem. Cut the tape in half lengthwise. Affix one half on the side seam of the right leg of the pants. Repeat for your left leg.

4 Keep the jacket unbuttoned.
Buttoning the jacket will make the improper fit more apparent.

5 | Distract with your cufflinks.
If the jacket sleeves are too short, make sure your cufflinks are of a high quality. Keep your arms slightly bent at all times to reduce the obviousness of the length disparity.

6 | Expand the shirt collar.
Loop a rubber band through the buttonhole of the shirt collar. Secure the ends to the collar button. Conceal with a necktie. Do not remove the tie during the wedding.

Split Seam

1 | Remove the jacket, shirt, or pants.

2 | Turn the garment inside out.

3 | Pull the seam together.
There will be a narrow section of fabric behind the seam. Pull the split sections together. Line up the sides carefully.

4 | Pin.
Using safety pins, connect the two sides. Pin the material as close to the seam as possible, but not so close that the pins will be visible from the outside.

5 | Check the repair.
Turn the garment right-side out. If the seam holds and the pins are not visible, the repair was successful. If the pins are visible, remove and start over.

Be Aware

• If no safety pins are available, use staples. Take care when removing them to prevent rips in the fabric. If neither pins nor staples are available, use electrical or duct tape. Fast-drying glue is also effective for repairing torn garments, but may damage or stain the fabric.

Lost Bow Tie

1 Make an emergency replacement from a cloth napkin.

• Place a well-starched white dinner napkin flat on a table in front of you. Using a pencil, carefully draw a circle about 1 inch in diameter.

• To the left of the circle, draw a triangle with sides about 2 inches long. One point of the triangle should extend slightly into the circle.

• Repeat, drawing a second triangle to the right of the circle, with one point extending into the circle. Your drawing should look like a bow tie when viewed from the front.

• Use scissors to cut the bow tie from the napkin. Turn the bow tie over so the pencil marks are on the back.

• Secure the cutout to your collar using loops of tape or safety pins. Do not wear with a black cummerbund: Make an emergency napkin cummerbund (see page 68) to match.

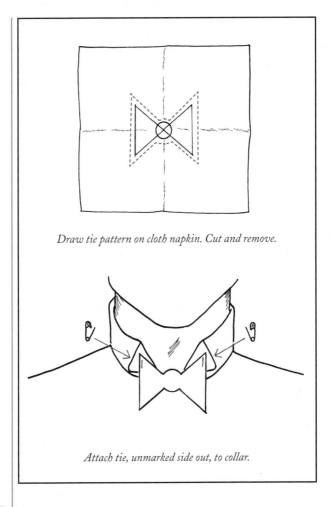

Draw tie pattern on cloth napkin. Cut and remove.

Attach tie, unmarked side out, to collar.

2 Wear a medallion.

Open your shirt at the collar and open three additional buttons. For a more fashionable look, borrow a spread collar shirt (one without a wing collar, which is made for a bow tie). Borrow and wear a large medallion, gold cross, Star of David, giant locket, or flashy pendant. To make a medallion:

- Open a wedding gift wrapped in gold-colored wrapping paper.
- Wrap the gold paper around a drink coaster or a similar-sized piece of cardboard. Cut the paper to fit, then tape or glue to cover.
- Affix your medallion to a black dress shoelace or piece of string with tape.
- Hang around your neck.

3 Make a bolo tie.

- Thread a black shoelace (leather or nylon) under and around your shirt collar to simulate a bolo lanyard.
- Run the two loose ends through the backing of a pin, pendant, or horizontal tie clasp.
- Slide the clasp up so it sits just below the second shirt button. Keep your collar button open.

Emergency Cuff Links

1 Remove your shirt.

2 Thread a narrow (1/8- to -inch-wide) ribbon through the cuff holes.
Leave the cuff open about half an inch. Do not tie the ends.

Emergency Cuff Links

shoelace

cherry stem

twist tie

3 | Tie knots.
On the outside of one cuff, tie a small knot on the ribbon as close to the hole as possible. Tie a second knot on top of the first.

4 | Check the knot diameter.
Test the knot by pulling gently on the other end of the ribbon. If the knot pulls through easily, tie another knot on top of the first two.

5 | Trim the ends.
When the knot is too big to fit through the hole easily, snip the excess ribbon just past the knot. Repeat on the other side of the cuff, then on the other sleeve. The knots may be pushed through the cuff holes after the shirt is on. They will hold the cuffs closed and look similar to braided silk cuff knots.

Be Aware

- Keep the jacket sleeve pulled down as far as possible to hide an unsightly fix.
- Items that can be used as emergency cuff links:
  - paper clips
  - twist ties
  - rubber bands
  - the metal rings from two key chains
  - large earrings
  - Maraschino cherry stems tied in knots
  - shoelaces (cut short)

Emergency Cummerbund

You will need a white cloth napkin for a white-tie wedding or a black or dark blue napkin for a black-tie event, plus a couple additional napkins to secure the cummerbund. The napkins should be starched and slightly stiff.

1 Place the napkin flat on a table in front of you, with one corner pointing toward you.

2 Fold the corner closest to you and the opposite corner into the center of the napkin.

3 Fold the bottom half of the napkin up toward the top edge.
The bottom edge should be about 1 inch above the top edge when the fold is complete.

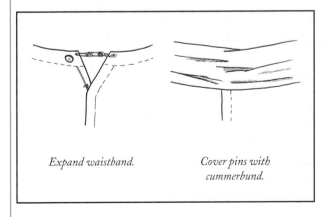

Expand waistband.

Cover pins with cummerbund.

4 | Fold both upper edges down toward the bottom edge. The lower of the two pleats should be one inch above the bottom edge. The napkin should now have three pleats and be the approximate shape of a cummerbund.

5 | Secure.
Tightly roll another napkin on the diagonal so it is long and thin. Tie or pin the second (or two more) napkin(s) to one end of the cummerbund, run it around your back, then tie or pin it to the other end. The pleats of the cummerbund should face up. Your jacket will obscure the sides of the napkin, even when unbuttoned.

PREVENT PERSPIRATION STAINS FROM SHOWING

1 | Wear an undershirt.
A thin cotton T-shirt will absorb sweat before it reaches your exterior layer of clothing.

2 | Wear perspiration shields.
Tape several layers of tissue paper, paper towels, or cocktail napkins to the underarm area of your shirt to absorb excess wetness. Do not use colored tissue or napkins because the ink from the dye may stain your shirt when wet.

3 | Wear chamois.
Cut a piece of chamois cloth, the ultra-absorbent cloth often employed for drying and polishing cars, into two

Elevate hand or soak ring finger in ice water to reduce swelling.

4-inch squares. Tape the squares to the underarm area of your shirt to remain extra dry.

4 | **Wear a pantiliner.**
Apply a self-sticking pantiliner or other feminine product to the underarm area of the shirt. Make sure you remove the product in private before joining your new spouse after the wedding.

Be Aware

- If you discover that the sweat has come through and is visible on your shirt, use a blow-dryer or hot-air hand dryer to dry the wet areas. It is not necessary to remove the shirt first.

HOW TO TREAT
A PANIC ATTACK

1 Realize that you're panicking.
Panic begets panic. Do not panic about panicking. Tell yourself that you are not dying or going crazy, but experiencing an anxiety attack. This awareness will prevent the attack from escalating.

2 Loosen your clothes.
Do not tear off your dress or jacket. Open a few buttons; lower a zipper.

3 Control your breathing.
Prevent hyperventilation by slowing your breathing. Breathe into a paper bag to restore a balance of oxygen and carbon dioxide in your lungs.

4 Distract yourself.
Focus on a physical object in the room. While breathing into the bag, close your eyes and try to recall the location and colors of all the objects in the room.

5 Act natural.
Open your eyes. Stop using the bag. Refasten zippers and buttons. Walk. Try to smile. Tell yourself it's over and everything is fine.

6 Resume your activities.

Control your breathing.

Be Aware
- An attack usually lasts between 15 and 30 minutes. Symptoms include pounding heart, sweating, dilated pupils, trembling, dry mouth, shortness of breath or sensation of being smothered, feelings of being choked, chest pain, nausea, dizziness, sense of being detached from oneself, and fear of losing control or going crazy.
- Knowing that you can conquer the attacks will sharply reduce their occurrence. Conversely, knowing that you are prey to attacks and cannot control them may sharply increase their occurrence.

HOW TO AVOID A NERVOUS BREAKDOWN BEFORE THE WEDDING

1 Ignore minor irritations.

Avoid driving at rush hour, upgrading your computer software, dealing with a governmental agency, thinking about your job, rooting for any sports team, undertaking a plumbing project, or listening to the local news.

2 Imagine yourself in a relaxing situation.

As you visualize, hold onto something tactile—a lucky rabbit's foot or your grandmother's favorite handkerchief. Hold it again later to restore your sense of calm. If you do not have a soothing object when the panic begins, conjure up safe and peaceful images.

3 Practice yoga.

Find a quiet room and close door. Dim the lights.

- Tree pose. Stand with your feet together. Draw your left foot up your right leg until it rests on your inner thigh. Put the palms of your hands together and raise them over your head. Balance and remain still. Lower your leg and repeat with the other side.
- Child's pose. Get on your hands and knees and sit back so that your bottom touches your heels and

Stress-Reducing Yoga Poses

tree pose   child's pose

your chest is resting on your thighs. Keep your arms
alongside your body with your fingers close to your
ankles and your cheek on the floor. Rest.

- Corpse pose. Remain on the floor. Turn over on
  your back. Rest your arms and legs flat on the floor.
  Close your eyes and relax every muscle. Do this for
  as long as it takes, but for at least 5 minutes. Do not
  fall asleep. Get up slowly when you feel calm, or
  when it is time to walk down the aisle.

4 | Laugh.
Rent videos of musicals from the 1930s, 1940s, and 1950s, especially those with Gene Kelly and Fred Astaire.

5 | Go to sleep early the night before the wedding.
Even if you cannot sleep, at least your body will be resting. Do not plan the bachelor or bachelorette party for the night before the ceremony.

6 | Eat and drink.
Make sure you eat on the big day, even if you do not feel hungry. Avoid caffeine, alcohol, and gassy, bloating foods. Remain hydrated. If you are prone to fainting, drink some juice, sugary soda, or a shot of grappa (for courage) before walking down the aisle.

7 | Elope.

Be Aware

- If something goes wrong, keep in mind that it will make for a hilarious story at anniversary parties.

HOW TO MAINTAIN COMPOSURE DURING THE CEREMONY

CRYING JAG

1 Take deep, measured breaths.
Inhale through your nose and exhale through your mouth. Deep breathing will calm you and prevent hyperventilation brought on by crying.

2 Stare at inanimate objects.
Focus on floral arrangements, your clothing, or the floor.

3 Recall trivial details.
Try to remember the color of your childhood blanket, or the make and model of all the cars you have owned. Attempt to say the alphabet or the months of the year backward.

4 Stand up straight.
Crying will cause you to bend forward and make your head and shoulders shake. Concentrate on good posture: Keep your back straight and your head held high to combat the physical effects of your emotions.

Be Aware
- Crying at weddings tends to be contagious and mutually reinforcing. Do not look at others who are crying or you may lose control.

LAUGHING FIT

1 Bite your tongue.
Bite down on your tongue hard enough to cause pain but not so hard that you cause bleeding or other injury.

2 Prick your finger.
Using the pin from your boutonniere or a thorn from a rose in your bouquet, quickly stick the pad of your thumb to cause pain. Put pressure on the pricked area for several minutes to avoid bloodstained clothing.

3 Pinch yourself.
The skin on the back of the upper arm is very sensitive. Squeeze a small section of skin between the thumb and index finger of your opposite hand. Release quickly to avoid a bruise.

4 Think about how much the wedding costs.

How to Avoid a Laughing Fit

Bite your tongue.

Prick your finger.

Pinch yourself.

Hiccups

1 Inhale through your mouth.

2 Hold your breath.

3 Slowly count to ten.

4 Swallow three times slowly.

5 Exhale.

6 Repeat.

Be Aware
- Swallow a flat (non-heaping) teaspoon or one paper packet of sugar in one quick gulp. Do not use a sugar substitute. Do not use salt.

Flatulence

1 Alter your stance.
Flatulence is more audible with the legs and buttocks close together. Shift your position so your feet are approximately 3 feet apart.

2 Sit down.

3 Shift the blame.
Look disapprovingly at a nearby guest or member of the bridal party. Do not look accusingly at your betrothed.

Standing on your head while drinking backward from a glass will not cure hiccups.

Be Aware

- Avoid introducing excess gas into your system. Do not smoke, chew gum, or drink carbonated beverages, and avoid beans, broccoli, cabbage, cauliflower, onions, and dairy products (if lactose intolerant) just before the ceremony.
- Chew activated charcoal tablets before the wedding. The charcoal will absorb odor caused by intestinal bacteria. Do not chew briquettes.

HOW TO SURVIVE IF SOMEONE OBJECTS

1   Laugh it off.
Smile, laugh, and keep things moving.

2   Make a joke.
If the protester persists, loudly exclaim, "Mom, it's going to be all right," or "I thought we were serving the liquor after the ceremony!"

3   Turn the crowd against the protester.
Say "This is the most important day of our lives, and we ask that you honor it with us."

4   Direct the best man to handle it.
If the guest continues to object, the best man should approach her, tell her quietly that she is disrupting the ceremony, and escort her out or to a side room, giving her the attention she craves.

5   Consider the objection in private.
If the protester might have a legitimate objecion (the groom is currently married to her), the best man should tell the bride, groom, and officiant, who should all discuss the matter before the ceremony continues.

Be Aware
* The consent of guests is not required for the marriage ceremony to be completed.

HOW TO BREAK UP
AN ARGUMENT

1 Speak to the offending guests softly and slowly.
Quietly tell them that their behavior is inappropriate
for a wedding, and that they must control themselves.
Do not raise your voice.

2 Reseat the guests.
If the argumentative guests are at the same table, ask
one to sit at another table.

3 Propose a toast.
As voices are being raised, begin tapping your glass
with a spoon to signal a toast. Other guests will follow
suit and the noise should drown out the shouting. The
argument will be put on hold during the toast, and
hopefully forgotten afterward—especially if the toast
is long and boring.

4 Stage a dance-off.
Clear the floor of other guests and have the band play
20 seconds for each fighting guest. Use an informal
survey of applause from other guests to determine the
victor.

5 Restrain the fighting guests.
If guests are coming to blows, enlist the help of burly
members of the wedding party or guests. Approach the

Ask feuding guests to settle their differences on the dance floor (audience applause determines the winner).

offending guests from behind and wrap each of them in a bear hug, with arms held firmly by their sides.

6 Propose a contest to resolve the dispute.
Seat combatants at a table that has been cleared. Let them pick between arm wrestling or thumb wrestling. Two out of three wins determines the victor.

7 Set up an outdoor competition
Ask the fighting guests to step outside. Explain that you are authorizing a race that will establish who wins the argument. Lay out a very long course.

HOW TO DEAL WITH LOST RINGS

1 Use cigar bands.
The best man or groomsmen may have cigars in their pockets. Slip the paper band off the cigar and give one to the bride and one to the groom to use in place of wedding bands. Large cigars with wide ring gauges have bands that are most likely to fit.

2 Borrow from guests.
Send the best man to collect rings from guests. Ask him to bring back an assortment of sizes so that one is sure to fit. The style of the ring does not matter.

3 Use a ponytail holder.
Twist the elastic in figure-8s until it is small enough to fit on a finger.

4 Bend paperclips.
Straighten and then bend the paperclips into a ring. Watch for sharp ends.

5 Braid rubber bands.
Braid three rubber bands, then tie loose ends together to form a ring.

How to Make an Emergency Ring

You will need the foil wrapper from a stick of chewing gum and a piece of tape. For a man's ring, use an entire wrapper; for a woman's ring, use a wrapper that has been cut in half lengthwise.

1 Remove the gum from the foil wrapper.
Discard or chew the gum.

2 Smooth the foil on a flat surface.
Flatten all wrinkles and folds.

3 Refold the wrapper lengthwise.
Follow the existing crease lines and fold each of the longer sides up to meet in the middle, leaving the short ends unfolded.

4 Fold the wrapper in half lengthwise.
The seams will be hidden in the middle.

5 Fold one end into a point.

6 Insert the point into the fold.

7 Fit the strip around your finger in the shape of a ring.
Size the ring to a comfortable fit.

8 Secure the ring with a small piece of tape.

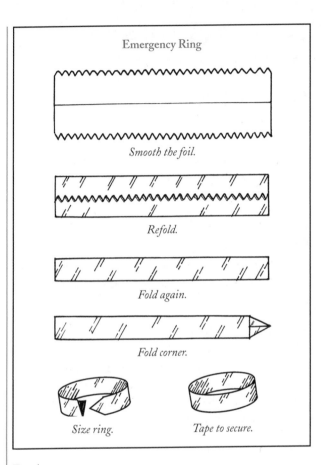

Emergency Ring

Smooth the foil.

Refold.

Fold again.

Fold corner.

Size ring.

Tape to secure.

Be Aware

- If a gum wrapper is not available, or if you prefer a different color ring, you can use paper money. Select foreign currencies for a more dramatic palate. Other options (cut to fit) include candy bar wrappers, aluminum foil, writing paper, or bank checks.

HOW TO DEAL WITH WEDDING NIGHT JITTERS

1 Eat.

You've probably been so busy and excited that you didn't have a chance to eat at the reception. Have some food now.

2 Postpone physical contact.

Unwind from the stress and excitement of the wedding before heading to the bedroom. Do something you both enjoy: Get an ice cream, take a stroll in a park, or just sit in a quiet place and talk about the day.

3 Eat mood-enhancing food.

Chocolate is an excellent mood enhancer: It contains the stimulants caffeine, theobromine, and phenylethylamine, as well as anandamide, a chemical—also produced naturally by the brain—that may enhance feelings of well-being.

4 Get the room ready.

Dim the lights, adjust the temperature, light scented candles, and put on soft music. Keep juices, bottled water, and fresh fruit on hand to rehydrate, rejuvenate, and reinvigorate.

5 Get yourselves set.
The bride and groom should be relaxed, comfortable, and confident. Offer a foot rub. Use lavender soap and scent to promote relaxation. Put on a cozy nightgown or robe over sexy lingerie or underwear.

6 Do something you've never done before.

How to Revive Your New Spouse

1 Brew coffee.
Pass a mug of coffee repeatedly under your spouse's nose.

2 Begin undressing your spouse.
Remove his socks to cool his body, then follow with his shirt, pants, and underwear. Most people will wake up if they sense they are being undressed.

3 Rub ice cubes over your spouse's body.
Start with the forehead, wrists, and soles of the feet. Keep going.

4 Apply pressure to the nail bed.
Take the tip of one of your spouse's fingers and hold it between your thumb and index finger. Very gently, apply steady pressure to the nail bed. Do not squeeze too hard. This method, used by emergency personnel to determine unconsciousness/unresponsiveness in victims, causes sharp pain. It should revive your partner quickly.

Reviving Your New Spouse

Use coffee.

Use his phone.

Use ice.

Use lung power.

5 | Tickle.

6 | Call on the telephone.
If you are in a hotel, call the front desk and ask them to ring your room. Or call your spouse's mobile phone from your mobile. Most people will respond to the sound of a ringing phone.

7 | Pretend there is an emergency.
Yell "Fire!" "Earthquake!" "Muggers!" and "Watch out!" repeatedly to get your spouse's adrenaline flowing. Once your spouse is awake, you can explain that you weren't ready for your special night together to end.

HOW TO SURVIVE A HONEYMOON DISASTER

EXTREME SUNBURN

1 Expose damaged skin to air.
Remove all clothing around the burn area: Clothing will irritate the burn site and may cause increased pain.

2 Drink water.
Drink at least 32 ounces of water to help promote sweating, which cools the skin.

3 Apply a cold compress.
Put ice in a plastic bag, wrap in a cotton T-shirt or other fabric, and apply to the burn area. If the burn area is very large, soak a bed sheet in ice water and apply it instead of a compress. Let the skin cool under the compress for 15 minutes to help reduce pain.

4 Apply a soothing gel or ointment to the burn area.
Carefully rub a cooling aloe lotion into the burned area. This is especially soothing if the aloe has been chilled in a refrigerator or a bucket of ice. Do not apply suntan lotion, baby oil, petroleum jelly, or any other foreign substance to the burn.

5 Take pain medication.
Ibuprofen will help reduce pain at the burn site.

6 Lie still.
Lie in a position that best exposes your sunburn to the air without coming into contact with the bed, your clothing, or another person. Do not bend sunburned joints.

7 Continue with your honeymoon.
Take advantage of loose-fitting island fashions as your sunburn heals.

Be Aware
• Depending on the severity of the sunburn, a new layer of skin will replace the burned area in two days to two weeks.

MIGRAINE HEADACHE

1 Dim the lights.
Bright lights may exacerbate a migraine or prolong symptoms. Keep the shades drawn and the room lights off or very low.

2 Reduce noise levels.
Turn off the radio and television. The room should be silent, or with soothing "white" noise such as that created by a small fan.

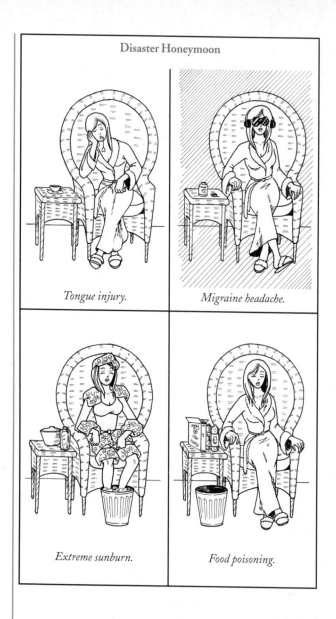

Disaster Honeymoon

Tongue injury.

Migraine headache.

Extreme sunburn.

Food poisoning.

3 | Limit movement.
Running, walking, and even climbing stairs may increase the intensity of a migraine.

4 | Eat vitamin-rich foods.
Magnesium and vitamin B2 (riboflavin) may combat migraine symptoms. Spinach, Swiss chard, and many nuts are high in magnesium, while mackerel, shad, and other oily fish are rich in riboflavin.

Be Aware
- A migraine may last as little as one hour or as long as three days.

ACUTE TONGUE INJURY

1 | Prepare a tea bag.
Soak a tea bag in warm water for 2 minutes. Let it stand 1 minute at room temperature, then wrap it in gauze or a clean cloth napkin.

2 | Apply tea bag to tongue.
Place the moist tea bag on the injury site and press steadily. The tannic acid in the tea is a natural coagulant and should stop the bleeding. The tongue has a large number of blood vessels near the surface and will bleed profusely until the blood coagulates.

3 | Rinse.
Swish and spit using an anesthetic mouthwash, if available.

4 | Apply a numbing agent.
Apply ice to the wound to numb and reduce pain.

5 | Avoid acidic and salty foods and liquids.
Acidic substances, such as citrus fruits and vinegar, and
those high in salt, such as nuts and potato chips, may
aggravate the injury.

6 | Keep the tongue still.
The tongue will heal more quickly if it is inactive.

7 | Protect the tongue.
Wear an athletic mouth guard to protect the tongue
until the injury heals.

Food Poisoning

1 | Stay hydrated.
Drink several gallons of water a day.

2 | Replenish mineral salts.
Nibble on dry salted crackers or plain rice to replace
salt lost through diarrhea.

3 | Do not induce vomiting.
Vomiting will not remove the bacterial culprit, but will
cause dehydration.

Be Aware

- Do not drink the water when traveling to the tropics or when you are unsure of its cleanliness. Avoid ice cubes in drinks, brushing your teeth with tap water, opening your mouth in the shower, or swallowing—or even rinsing your mouth with—water in swimming pools or the ocean.

- Only eat fruit that you can peel yourself. Avoid all vegetables and fruits that could have been washed in contaminated water, or fruits (like melons) that might have been soaked in water to increase their size and weight.

- If you don't know what it is, don't eat it.

HOW TO
DELIVER A BABY
IN A TAXICAB

Before you attempt to deliver a baby, use your best
efforts to get to a hospital first. There really is no way
to know exactly when the baby is ready to emerge, so
even if you think you may not have time to get to the
hospital, you probably do. Even the "water breaking"
is not a sure sign that birth will happen immediately. The water is actually the amniotic fluid and the
membrane that the baby floats in; birth can occur
many hours after the mother's water breaks. However,
if you leave too late or get stuck in crosstown traffic
and you must deliver the baby on your own, here are
the basic concepts.

1 Time the uterine contractions.
For first-time mothers, when contractions are about
three to five minutes apart and last forty to ninety seconds—and increase in strength and frequency—for at
least an hour, the labor is most likely real and not false
(though it can be). Babies basically deliver themselves,
and they will not come out of the womb until they are
ready. Have clean, dry towels, a clean shirt, or something similar on hand.

As the baby moves through
the birth canal, guide it out
by supporting the head.

Support the body as it moves
out. Do not slap its behind
to make it cry; the baby
will breathe on its own.

After you have dried off the baby, tie the umbilical cord with
a shoelace or a piece of string several inches from the body.
Leave the cord alone until the baby gets to the hospital.

2 As the baby moves out of the womb, its head—the biggest part of its body—will open the cervix so the rest of it can pass through.

(If feet are coming out first, see next page.) As the baby moves through the birth canal and out of the mother's body, guide it out by supporting the head and then the body.

3 When the baby is out of the mother, dry it off and keep it warm.

Do not slap its behind to make it cry; the baby will breathe on its own. If necessary, clear any fluid out of the baby's mouth with your fingers.

4 Tie off the umbilical cord.

Take a piece of string—a shoelace works well—and tie off the cord several inches from the baby.

5 It is not necessary to cut the umbilical cord, unless you are hours away from the hospital.

In that event, you can safely cut the cord by tying it in another place a few inches closer to the mother and cutting it between the knots. Leave the cord alone until you get to a hospital. The piece of the cord attached to the baby will fall off by itself. The placenta will follow the baby in as few as three or as many as thirty minutes.

The most common complication during pregnancy is a breech baby, or one that is positioned so the feet, and not the head, will come out of the uterus first. Since the head is the largest part of the baby, the danger is that, if the feet come out first, the cervix may not be dilated enough to get the head out afterward. Today, most breech babies are delivered through cesarean sections, a surgical procedure that you will not be able to perform. If you have absolutely no alternatives (no hospital or doctors or midwives are available) when the baby begins to emerge, you can try to deliver the baby feet first. A breech birth does not necessarily mean that the head won't be able to get through the cervix; there is simply a higher possibility that this will occur. Deliver the baby as you would in the manner prescribed above.

HOW TO SURVIVE IF YOU FORGET YOUR ANNIVERSARY

1 Order an emergency bouquet.
Many florists can assemble arrangements with little notice. If you have just minutes to prepare, scour your neighborhood flowerbeds for daisies. Wrap them in colorful ribbon and present them as your initial gift.

2 Buy chocolates.
Most supermarkets and drugstores carry chocolate assortments. Choose a tasteful boxed set rather than several loose candy bars tied with ribbon.

3 Create a voucher card.
Prepare a card or piece of paper that shows the wonderful gift you're giving but can't give now because it isn't ready yet. Draw a picture of the gift on the card or paper.

4 Apologize, apologize, apologize.
If you're caught with nothing, making excuses will not help your case. Your level of contrition should be so extreme that your spouse begins to feel bad because you feel so terrible.

5 Give an intangible present.
Give her a homemade certificate for a weekend spa getaway. It could be for her only, or for a romantic weekend for both of you—a "second honeymoon" (but don't push your luck). A week free of household chores, a weekend of breakfasts in bed, or getting her car detailed are other possibilities.

How to Sleep on the Couch

1 Remove the back cushions.
If the couch has loose back cushions, take them off to add more width to the sleeping surface.

2 Remove the arm cushions.
Side cushions take up precious head and leg room, and will just end up on the floor in the middle of the night anyway.

3 Fluff and flip.
If the sofa design permits, remove the seat cushions, fluff them, then flip them so the side that was down is now the top. This will provide a more even sleeping surface.

4 Cover the seat cushions with a sheet.
The sheet will protect your face from odors trapped in the cushions and will protect the seating area from saliva.

5 Use your usual pillow.
You will sleep better with your head resting on a familiar pillow. Get yours from the bedroom, if the bedroom is still accessible to you.

6 Depending on the temperature of the room and your comfort level, get a sheet, blanket, comforter, or large towel to put on top of you.

7 Relax.
Do not to go to bed angry.

Be Aware

- If you are an active sleeper, lay the sofa cushions next to the sofa to break your fall should you roll off during the night.

WEDDING SURVIVAL CHECKLISTS

Make sure you have these items.

Walking-Down-the-Aisle Survival Checklist

- ❑ Bride
- ❑ Veil
- ❑ Wedding dress
- ❑ Shoes (hers)
- ❑ Maid of honor
- ❑ Bridesmaids
- ❑ Someone to give the bride away
- ❑ Groom
- ❑ Tuxedo/suit
- ❑ Shoes (his)
- ❑ Best man
- ❑ Rings
- ❑ Petroleum jelly (in case ring won't fit)
- ❑ Chewing gum (use wrappers to make emergency rings)
- ❑ Groomsmen
- ❑ Officiant
- ❑ Emergency vows (in case officiant forgets)
- ❑ Small paper bag (to alleviate hyperventilation)
- ❑ Flask with alcohol (for courage)
- ❑ Tranquilizers
- ❑ Smelling salts

Reception Survival Checklist

- ❏ Food
- ❏ Liquor
- ❏ Place to put presents
- ❏ Formal gloves (to block reception line germs)
- ❏ Butter (to soothe chapped lips from kissing)
- ❏ Photographer
- ❏ Garter
- ❏ Scarf (to use as emergency garter)
- ❏ Tables
- ❏ Chairs
- ❏ Napkins
- ❏ Cake
- ❏ Band
- ❏ Small car with loud sound system (to replace missing band)
- ❏ Petroleum jelly (apply to insteps for gliding dance moves)
- ❏ Duct tape and shot glasses (to replace shoe heel)
- ❏ Electrical tape (to make tuxedo stripe on pants)
- ❏ Insect repellant (for outdoor weddings)
- ❏ Tranquilizers
- ❏ Smelling salts

Honeymoon Survival Checklist

- ❑ Airline tickets
- ❑ Toothbrushes
- ❑ Toothpaste
- ❑ Straw hats (for hot climates)
- ❑ Hats with earflaps (for cold climates)
- ❑ Insect repellant (for tropical climates)
- ❑ Flashlight
- ❑ Sunscreen
- ❑ Aloe (to treat sunburn)
- ❑ Aspirin (for headaches)
- ❑ Ice pack (for headaches, sunburns, and sprains)
- ❑ Tea bags (to soothe swollen eyes and tongue)
- ❑ Petroleum jelly
- ❑ Bottled water (for sunburn, upset stomach)
- ❑ Antacids (for upset stomach)
- ❑ Club soda (for upset stomach)
- ❑ Crackers (for upset stomach)
- ❑ Sexy lingerie
- ❑ Smelling salts
- ❑ Tranquilizers

APPENDIX

THE "IT'S NOT YOU, IT'S ME" LETTER

Dear _____ ,

I won't be able to make it this Saturday, or any Saturday, in fact. The truth is, I just can't be in a committed relationship right now. It's not you, it's me. I'm just not able to appreciate all that you have to give.

I feel like we've been spinning our wheels these last few years / months / weeks / days. I can't believe how wonderful you've been to me and how much you've put up with. You deserve better. I can't put you through this anymore and I can't give you what you need / want / deserve right now. I need more space, and I need time to figure out who the real [your name here] is.

It may take some time, but I hope we can still be friends.

Sincerely,

[your name here]

For short-term relationships, this letter may be sent via fax or e-mail. To download the latest version, visit www.worstcasescenarios.com.

USEFUL EXCUSES

- This never happened to me before.
- I had a really tough day at work.
- Not tonight, I have a meeting.
- I have to get up early.
- I'm too drunk.
- I'm not drunk enough.
- My turtle died.
- I'm gay.
- I'm straight.
- I can't decide.
- It's an old football injury.
- I forgot my wallet.
- I have to wash my hair.
- My Aunt Flo is visiting.
- I am leaving the country.
- I need to take my medication.
- I couldn't find a place to park.
- I couldn't get a cab.
- I left it in the cab.
- I have to catch a plane.
- I buy it for the articles.

- They're supposed to test them at the factory.
- Nobody's perfect.
- I warned you about me.
- We don't know each other well enough.
- We know each other too well for that.
- I didn't think you were coming back today.
- He/she needed a friend.
- It meant nothing to me.
- Someone told me it was an art film.
- We might learn some new things from it.
- I have a bad back.
- I have bad knees.
- I asked you first.
- I have to walk my dog.
- That's not what I meant.
- I don't remember saying that.
- I'm terrible with names.
- I can't bend over that far.
- I didn't think you would notice.
- My pager is broken.
- My cell phone needs recharging.
- My computer has a virus.
- Your voicemail was full.

PICKUP LINES TO AVOID (OR USE)

- The human body is 90 percent water, and I'm real thirsty.

- Can I buy you a drink or do you just want the money?

- With a mane like that you must be a Leo.

- Do you have a mirror in your pants? Because I can see myself in them.

- Are your legs tired? Because you have been running through my dreams all night.

- Is your father a thief? He has stolen the stars from the skies and put them in your eyes.

- Are you okay? It must have been a long fall from heaven.

- I really like that outfit. It would look great crumpled at the end of my bed.

- What do you like to eat for breakfast? Oh good, I have that.

- I know they say milk does a body good—but damn, how much have you been drinking?

- So, are you legal?

- I have cable TV.

- If I told you that you have a lovely body, would you hold it against me?

- Did the sun just come out or did you smile at me?

- Is it hot in here, or is it just you?

- Do you believe in love at first sight or do I have to walk by you again?

- Hey, I lost my phone number . . . can I have yours?

- If you were a burger at McDonald's, I'd call you McBeautiful.

- Hi, my name's _____ . But you can call me . . . tonight.

- No wonder the sky's gray today—all the blue is in your eyes.

- What's your name? Or shall I just call you mine?

- If I could rearrange the alphabet, I'd put U and I together.

- Look at you with all those curves and me with no brakes!

- I may not be Fred Flintstone/Wilma Flintstone, but I can sure make your bed rock!

- Do you have any raisins? No? How about a date?

- Do you have a Band-Aid? 'Cause I skinned my knee when I fell for you.

- Can I have a picture of you so I can show Santa what I want for Christmas?

- My bed is broken. Can I sleep in yours?

- I'm not feeling myself tonight. Can I feel you?

- My name is _____ . Remember that; you'll be screaming it later.

- Is that a ladder in your stockings or the stairway to heaven?

- I may not be the best looking guy/girl in here, but I'm the only one talking to you.

- (Lick finger and wipe on his/her shirt.) Let's get you out of these wet clothes.

GUIDE TO BODY LANGUAGE

Good Signs

- Leans in = receptiveness

- Legs slightly apart = attraction

- Makes good eye contact = sincerity

- Matches your breathing = a meeting of the minds

- Moves when you do = a good match

- Holds palms open = receptiveness, an invitation

- Parts lips = desire

- Smiles with crow's feet = genuine amusement, attraction

- Touches face, cheek = interest, attraction

- Touches you = desire, attraction

- Twirls hair = attraction, flirtation

- Unbuttons jacket or shirt = comfort, interest

Parts lips = desire

Unbuttons jacket or shirt =
comfort, interest

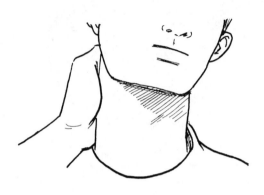

Rubs neck or head = impatience, frustration

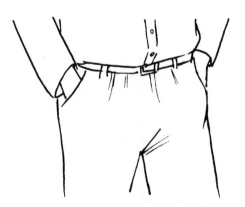

Shoves hands in pockets = feelings of
inadequacy or insecurity, disinterest

Bad Signs

⭐ Clenches jaw = impatience, anger

⭐ Crosses legs or arms = defensiveness

⭐ Holds finger to chin or lips = evaluation, criticism

⭐ Looks around = disinterest, boredom

⭐ Looks away = insincerity

⭐ Nods too much = disinterest, short attention span

⭐ Rubs neck or head = impatience, frustration

⭐ Rubs nose or eyes =
dismissal, readiness to move on

⭐ Shifts weight = uncertainty, nervousness

⭐ Shoves hands in pockets =
feelings of inadequacy or insecurity, disinterest

⭐ Slouches = boredom, disinterest

⭐ Smiles without crow's feet =
an attempt to look happy

"BIRDS-AND-BEES" SPEECH

Son/Daughter,

I think you're old enough now to understand some things about Nature and how we all got here. It's best that you hear about these things from me and not from the kids at school who might not understand everything. I'll explain things to you, and you can talk to me without feeling embarrassed.

You've noticed that there are differences between boys and girls, between moms and dads, and soon you will notice that your body is changing. These changes are normal, and have to do with hormones that your body produces. These hormones and changes are the way your body gets ready to become an adult and to be able to make a baby.

It takes both a man and a woman to make a baby, just the way it takes a male dog and a female dog to make puppies. The female has a litter, which means she gives birth to several tiny puppies at the same time. Other animals have babies by laying eggs, but it still takes a male chicken, called a rooster, and a female chicken, called a hen, to produce eggs that have chicks inside. Hens can produce eggs without a rooster, like the eggs we have for breakfast, but those eggs aren't fertilized, which means that they don't have a chick inside and they won't hatch. All birds lay eggs. Female bees and fish also lay eggs, but the way the male fertilizes the eggs is different.

I think that's enough for one day.

Any questions?

ACKNOWLEDGMENTS

David Borgenicht would like to thank his amazing co-authors, Ben Winters, Josh Piven, and Jennifer Worick, his editor Steve Mockus, as well as the crew at Quirk (Jason Rekulak, Erin Slonaker, Mary Ellen Wilson, and Mandy Sampson) who worked on this book. You make book-making as easy as falling in love. Mostly, however, he'd like to thank all of his ex-girlfriends and bad dates for enduring his indulgences in his quest for love and sex. It was always him, not you. Finally, he would like to thank his wife, Suzanne Simons, for finally taking him off the market.

ABOUT THE AUTHORS

- **David Borgenicht** is a writer and publisher who lives with his family in Philadelphia. He is the coauthor of all the books in the *Worst-Case Scenario Survival Handbook* series.

- **Brenda Brown** is an illustrator and cartoonist whose work has been published in many books and publications, including the *Worst-Case Scenario* series, *Esquire*, *Reader's Digest*, *USA Weekend*, *21st Century Science & Technology*, the *Saturday Evening Post*, and the *National Enquirer*. Her Web site is www.webtoon.com

- **Sarah Jordan** is coauthor of *The Worst-Case Scenario Survival Handbook: Parenting* and *The Worst-Case Scenario Survival Handbook: Weddings*.

- **Joshua Piven** is the coauthor, along with David Borgenicht, of all the *Worst-Case Scenario Survival Handbooks*. He lives in Philadelphia with his family.

- **Turk Regan** is the co-author of The Worst-Case Scenario Almanac: Politics.

- **Victoria De Silverio** is coauthor of *The Worst-Case Scenario Pocket Guide: Breakups.*

- **Sam Stall** is coauthor of *The Worst-Case Scenario Pocket Guide: Dogs.*

- **Ben H. Winters** is coauthor of *The Worst-Case Scenario Pocket Guides* for *Cars, Cats, Meetings, New York City,* and *San Francisco.*

- **Jennifer Worick** is coauthor of *The Worst-Case Scenario Survival Handbook: College* and *The Worst-Case Scenario Survival Handbook: Dating & Sex.*

THE COMPLETE
WORST-CASE SCENARIO
SURVIVAL HANDBOOKS

Each of these comprehensive, indestructible handbooks is jam-packed with illustrated survival scenarios and expert advice to keep you safe in any situation.

THE ULTIMATE
WORST-CASE SCENARIO
SURVIVAL HANDBOOK

This ultimate large-format collection features 400 scenarios from all twenty-six titles of the world's bestselling survival handbook series for the first time, plus dozens of new entries.

THE FIRST OF THE WORST

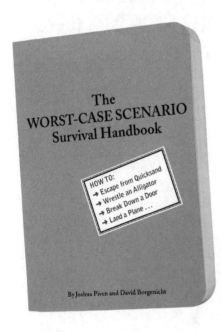

The
WORST-CASE SCENARIO
Survival Handbook

HOW TO:
→ Escape from Quicksand
→ Wrestle an Alligator
→ Break Down a Door
→ Land a Plane ...

By Joshua Piven and David Borgenicht

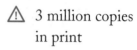 3 million copies in print

⚠ Translated into 27 languages

⚠ International best-seller

"An armchair guide for the anxious."
—*USA Today*

"The book to have when the killer bees arrive."
—*The New Yorker*

"Nearly 180 pages of immediate action drills for when everything goes to hell in a handbasket."
—*Soldier of Fortune*

"This is a really nifty book."
—*Forbes*

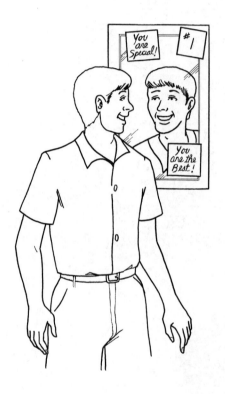